Jenny Ridgwell & Judy Ridgway

FOOD
AROUND THE WORLD

Oxford University Press

Oxford University Press, Walton Street, Oxford OX2 6DP

Oxford New York Toronto
Delhi Bombay Calcutta Madras Karachi
Petaling Jaya Singapore Hong Kong Tokyo
Nairobi Dar es Salaam Cape Town
Melbourne Auckland

and associated companies in
Berlin Ibadan

Oxford is a trade mark of Oxford University Press

ISBN 0 19 832728 5 (limp, non-net)
ISBN 0 19 832727 7 (cased, net)

Acknowledgements

*The publisher would like to thank the following for permission to reproduce
their photographs:*

Heather Angel p. 61 (bottom), p. 80, p. 108; Apple and Pear
Development p. 9 (right); BPCC/Aldus Archive p. 121 (left); Bridgeman
Art Library p. 30 (top); Camera Press p. 15 (right); Roger Charlesson
p. 121 (right); CMA – German Food and Drink p. 40; Bruce Coleman
p. 8, p. 13 (top), p. 39 (top), p. 52, p. 59 (right), p. 68, p. 92 (right),
p. 96 (top), p. 97, p. 117; Collins Publishers/Quick and Easy Indian
Cooking by Michael Pandya p. 75; Colour Library International p. 27
(right), p. 59 (left), p. 87 (left); Danish Dairy Board p. 14; James Davis
Library p. 96 (bottom); DFDS p. 13 (bottom); Ente Nazionale Italiano
per il Turismo p. 31 (top); ET Archive p. 51; Mary Evans Picture
Library p. 98 (bottom), p. 99 (top); Food and Wine from France p. 18;
Format p. 58, p. 90, p. 92 (left); John Garrett p. 32 (top), p. 44; Sally
and Richard Greenhill p. 76 (left and right), p. 77, p. 78; John and
Penny Hubley p. 72, p. 105; Hutchison p. 61 (top), p. 62; JPNTO p. 86,
p. 89; Rob Judges p. 15 (left), p. 32 (middle), p. 39 (bottom), p. 43
(right); Kelloggs p. 99 (bottom); Marshall Cavendish p. 24; Tony
Morrison p. 116; Multi Media/Maggie Murray p. 104; National Dairy
Council p. 9 (left); Network p. 60, p. 120 (left and right); Peter Newark's
Western Americana p. 98 (top); Pickthall Picture Library p. 91; Seaphot
p. 87 (bottom right); Sharwoods p. 67 (left and right); Sheffield City
Museums p. 32 (bottom); John Sims p. 26; Spanish Promotion Centre
p. 27 (left); Spectrum p. 30 (bottom); Sally Stradling p. 19; Turkish
Tourist Board p. 45 (top).

Illustrations are by Nancy Anderson, Ann Baum, Pat Capon, Vanessa
Luff and Nigel Paige.

Cover photographs and interior recipe photographs are by Steven Lee.

The authors would like to thank the following people who helped to
check the manuscript:
Anne-Marie Bertin, Kersten Burge, Izumi Dumont, Beryl Farla, Gila
Godsi, Sara Godsi, Anne Legg, John Legg, Mary Stewart, Evelyn
Willcock, Berooz Yazdani, and Luke Daniels.

Set by Graphicraft Typesetters Limited Hong Kong
Printed in Hong Kong

CONTENTS

INTRODUCTION

It is fascinating to learn about other people's foods and eating habits. There is so much to discover that is both interesting and useful. New ingredients are constantly arriving in the shops, familiar foods can be prepared in entirely different ways, and most important, the diet of other cultures may be more nutritious and healthy than that in the West.

People who eat a diet with enough cereals such as rice, maize, or wheat, and beans, nuts, fruits, and vegetables, seem to be healthier, stronger, and live longer. Most people who live in the so-called 'developed countries' eat a lot more meat and dairy foods, other fatty foods and sugar, and less cereals, fruits, and vegetables, including roots and tubers.

Foods eaten in industrial countries

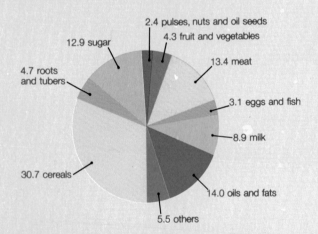

Foods eaten in developing countries

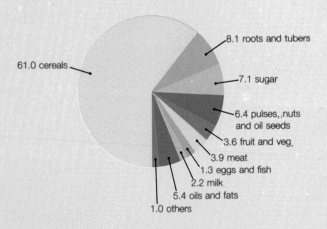

The two pie charts show the comparison between foods eaten in a developed industrial country such as Britain, and the diet of developing countries. Notice how the developing country eats twice as much cereal as the developed country does, but much less meat and dairy foods.

WHERE FOOD GROWS

Of course, food is not evenly distributed around the world. Some mountainous areas of South America or jungle regions in South-East Asia are just not suitable for growing food. Different crops thrive in particular climates and soil conditions, and on particular types of land.

Rice grows in hot, rainy areas, usually in flooded fields called paddies. Although wheat is grown all over the world, it grows best in temperate areas and needs moist, cool days to start with, then dry, sunny days for ripening and harvesting.

The area between the Tropic of Cancer and the Tropic of Capricorn is warm or very hot throughout the year. Tropical fruits and vegetables will only grow in this region. These include pineapples, mangoes, bananas, plantains, yams, and cassava.

STAPLE FOODS

Foods which grow well in an area and are eaten in quantity because they are plentiful and cheap become the staple food of the people living there.

Rice is a staple food in parts of India, China, and Indonesia. Wheat is the staple food in temperate areas such as the USA and Europe. Cassava root is an important food in areas of Africa and the West Indies, and maize plays a major role in the diet of people from Central and South America.

◀ *World Food Survey, Food and Agricultural Organization*

THE WORLD FOOD BALANCE

Some countries, through natural disasters such as drought, or because of poverty, wars, or poor farming methods, cannot provide enough food for their people. Many people in these countries suffer from undernourishment or even die from starvation.

On the other hand, people in other countries may eat too much and choose the wrong kind of food. Diseases related to food include obesity, heart disease, diabetes, and dental decay.

Food is essential to provide us with energy. The energy value of food is measured in units called kilocalories. Each person's energy requirement is different depending upon how old they are, whether they are male or female, and how active they are. An energetic teenager will have a higher energy requirement than an older person who sits in an office all day. The chart below shows the energy requirements of different people.

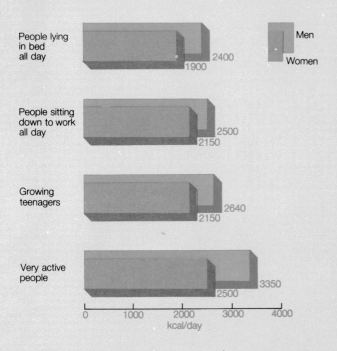

Some people of the world consume more food than they need whereas others eat too little. This bar chart shows the average daily intake of

kilocalories of people in different countries.

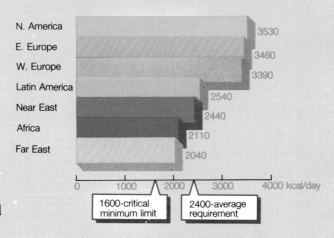

LOOKING AT FOOD AROUND THE WORLD

In this book, countries are arranged in a round-the-world trip, starting with Britain. Some countries such as Hungary, Germany, and Austria fall into natural groups with a common history and similar foods and cooking methods. Other areas like Spain, France, and Italy, although geographically close, have very different ways of preparing food and so each need a separate chapter. The trip ends with a section on Jewish cooking. Jewish people have travelled throughout the world and their history is reflected in their special foods.

One way to begin to find out what is eaten in a region is to look at what crops and animals are farmed and reared. Scandinavia has a large fishing industry and grows rye, so fish is an important food and a lot of rye is eaten in the form of bread and crispbreads. Maize is the most important cereal grown in Mexico. Ground maize is used to make the pancake-like tortillas, eaten with every meal. Many types of chilli pepper are grown in Mexico and are used along with tomatoes to give food a spicy hotness and colour.

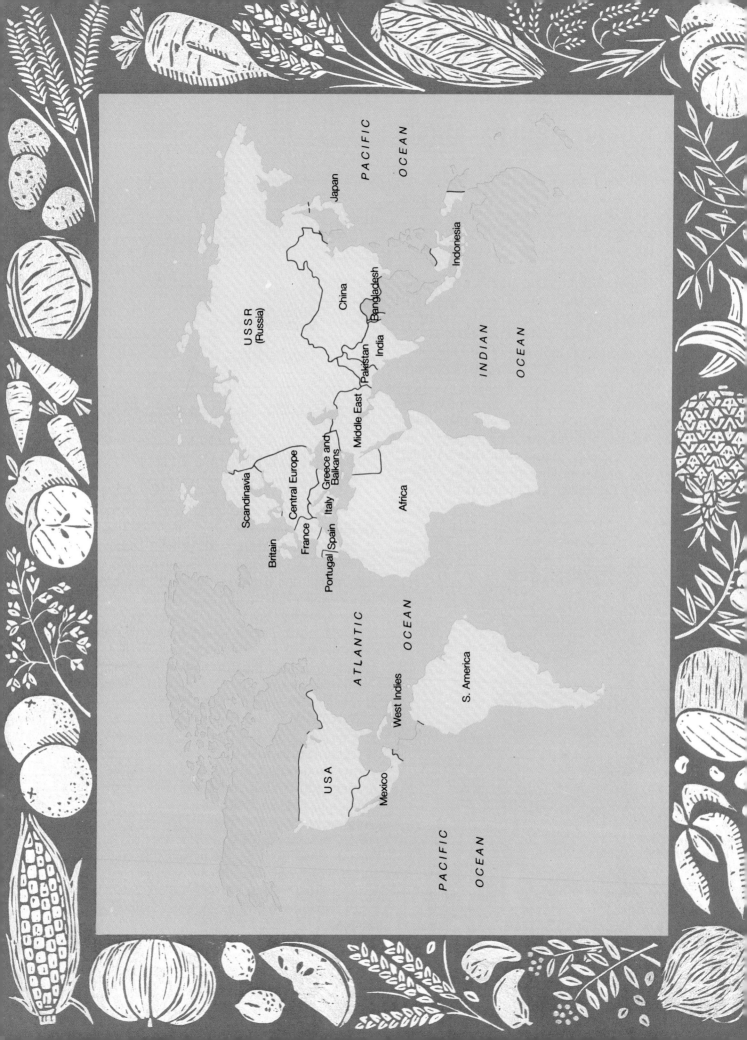

The history of an area plays a major role too. The Arabs took oranges, rice, almonds, and spices to Spain and greatly changed the type of food served there. Breadfruit, sugar cane, and mangoes were all taken to the West Indies by various settlers and later became valuable food crops there.

Different cultures use the same ingredients to make entirely different dishes. Tomatoes, which were discovered in South America and now thrive far from their country of origin, are used to make the famous Spanish soup, gazpacho, to provide toppings for Italian pizzas, and to flavour sauces for Indian curries.

It is interesting to look at the pattern of daily meals in other countries. In hot areas such as Spain, people often have a long lunch late in the day to avoid working in the heat of the afternoon. Few countries, apart from those in northern Europe and North America, eat a pudding at the end of a meal. Fresh fruit is often eaten instead. The traditional diet and meal pattern of many countries such as Britain and Japan is changing with the introduction of fast foods such as hamburgers, breakfast cereals, and soft drinks.

THE RECIPES

The selection of recipes included in this book has been carefully made. Traditional dishes have been chosen, using where possible the foods of the country concerned. Occasionally alterations have been made. It is important to remember that what is a cheap food in one country may be very expensive in another. Yams, cassava, and plantains are cheap foods in the Tropics, but their price increases when they are exported great distances.

The cost of food is an important consideration. Delicious dishes do not need expensive ingredients. Sometimes, however, special items may be essential to give the right flavour to a dish – tahina for example, used in hummus, or salt cod fish for West Indian food – and these may be relatively expensive.

The original recipe may have been slightly adapted in order to use less fat, sugar, red meat, or dairy produce, and more cereals, fruit, or vegetables, to fit in with modern dietary guidelines.

Cooking time has been considered, and most dishes can be prepared and cooked within one hour or else can be left to cook unattended.

HOW TO USE THE RECIPES

1 Use plain flour unless otherwise stated.
2 Use size 3 eggs.
3 Freshly ground black pepper tastes best.
4 Buy fresh spices for recipes if possible, as ground spice loses its flavour after a time.
5 Polyunsaturated vegetable oil, e.g. sunflower oil, is considered healthier to use in cooking than saturated fats such as butter and lard.
6 Buy lean meat where possible.
7 Wholemeal flour and brown rice may be substituted for white flour and rice in some recipes to increase dietary fibre. However, the dishes will no longer be traditional.
8 Can sizes. As can sizes vary, the approximate weight has been given. Simply buy the can nearest to this weight.
9 Some people do not like garlic, olives, and hot, spicy food. The first two can be left out and the chilli pepper or curry powder cut down to make a dish less hot.

ABBREVIATIONS USED

tsp	teaspoon
tbs	tablespoon
ml	millilitre
g	gram
cm	centimetre

Do try out food from other countries. There is so much to learn and enjoy. Find out more about the food you eat. Information is everywhere – look around when shopping, read labels and newspapers, but above all ask people – you may be surprised what they know.

BRITAIN

Fifty-six million people live in Britain. The country cannot grow enough food to feed everyone, so much is imported. However, agriculture is highly successful in Britain. For centuries East Anglian grain fields have had the highest yield per acre in Europe. Important crops include barley, wheat, potatoes, and sugar beet. Livestock farming is important too. Chickens and turkeys are the most popular animals with over one billion reared each year. Sheep, then cattle, are the next largest groups.

With greater opportunities for travel and more people from all parts of the world coming to live in Britain, British eating habits are changing. Most people have tried Chinese and Indian food as well as pastas, pizzas, and American hamburgers. Traditional British dishes are being replaced by new cooking ideas.

SOME BRITISH FOODS

BREAD

Bread has always been an important food in Britain. Today bread is made from wheat flour but in the past rye, oats, and barley were mixed in to make a cheaper, coarser bread.

White bread is popular, but many minerals and vitamins as well as fibre are lost in the milling process. Today more and more people are realizing the benefits of eating wholemeal flour which has had nothing taken away, so no nutrients are lost.

MEAT

Roast beef, roast potatoes, and Yorkshire pudding is a traditional Sunday lunch. However, beef is expensive and people are now eating less meat as well as choosing chicken and turkey or cheaper cuts of lamb and pork instead of beef.

FISH

Although the islands are surrounded by sea, people eat less fish nowadays than they did in the past. Some fish is smoked, which in the past helped the fish to keep well. Popular smoked fish includes cod, salmon, and herring. The latter are called kippers when smoked. Fish farms now produce fish such as trout, and shellfish like oysters.

Seafish and shellfish caught by a trawler off Plymouth

BACON

For over 700 years British people have been eating bacon and they now eat more than any other nation. Bacon is made from fresh pork, soaked in salt solution for a few days, then left to mature. The pale pink bacon produced in this way is called green bacon. Smoked bacon is darker in colour.

CHEESES

Cheese has been made for hundreds of years in Britain and other countries have copied British cheese-making recipes, especially for Cheddar cheese.

Cox's orange pippins

APPLES AND PEARS

Since Mediaeval times apples and pears have been grown in Britain, especially in the orchards of Kent, Herefordshire, and East Anglia. The Bramley apple is a delicious cooking apple which is grown commercially only in Britain. Other countries use dessert apples for cooking. Cox's Orange Pippin is one of the best crisp and juicy eating apples grown in Britain.

Conference and Comice are well-known pears. Conference got its name because it won first prize at a Pear Conference in 1885. It is dark green and sometimes hard. Comice is yellowish with a sweet juicy flesh.

DID YOU KNOW?

In Britain the turkey used to be eaten only at Christmas. In the eighteenth century birds were marched, wearing special boots, from Norfolk to London to be sold for Christmas dinner. The largest turkey farm in the world is in Norfolk, with seven million birds.

The Earl of Sandwich was too busy gambling to sit down to eat at the dinner table. He asked for his roast beef to be sent between two slices of bread and so invented the first sandwich.

CHEESE AND HERB ◀ LOAF ▶

This loaf is made from baking powder instead of traditional yeast. It is delicious served warm with soups and salads.

225 g wholewheat flour
3 level tsp baking powder
1 tsp dried mustard
pinch of salt
25 g butter *or* margarine
2 level tsp dried mixed herbs
75 g strong cheese, grated
1 egg
120 ml milk

1 Set the oven at 190°C/375°F/Gas 5 and grease a medium loaf tin.
2 Sieve the flour, baking powder, mustard, and salt into a bowl. Shake in the bran from the sieve. Cut the butter into pieces and rub into the flour using your fingertips. Add the cheese and herbs.
3 Whisk the egg and milk together and beat into the flour. Put the mixture into the tin and smooth down. Bake for 40–45 minutes until firm.
4 Turn out and cool on a wire rack.

Serves 4–6.

CREAMY CARROT ◀ SOUP ▶

The early carrot was purple and came to England from Afghanistan! Carrots were once so exotic that ladies of the court pinned the feathery green tops to their hats.

700 g carrots, washed and scraped
1 large potato, peeled
1 onion, peeled
25 g butter *or* 1 tbs vegetable oil
1 level tbs flour
700 ml water
150 ml milk
$\frac{1}{2}$ tsp each of salt and pepper
a little grated nutmeg and chopped parsley

1 Grate the carrot, potato, and onion. Fry them gently in a pan in the butter or oil.
2 After 5 minutes add the flour and stir. Add the water, milk, salt, and pepper. Boil, then cover and simmer for 20 minutes.
3 Serve decorated with a sprinkling of nutmeg and parsley.

Serves 4.

FLUFFY BACON AND
◀ APPLE OMELETTE ▶

Bacon and apples are old English foods. The Romans introduced mustard to Britain.

3 eggs
1 tbs water
25 g butter *or* 1 tbs oil
2 rashers of bacon, diced
1 eating apple, cored and diced
pinch of mustard powder

1 Fry the bacon and apple gently together until the bacon is tender – there is no need to use extra fat.
2 Separate the eggs. Just take the tip from the pointed end of the egg, using a knife. Let the white slip out into a clean bowl and put the yolk into a separate bowl. Separate each egg like this, then mix the yolks with the water and in the other bowl beat the whites until stiff. Finally, fold the whites into the yolks.
3 Heat the butter in a large omelette pan. Pour in the egg mixture and leave to cook for $2-2\frac{1}{2}$ minutes. Spread over the bacon and apple and sprinkle on some mustard.
4 Stand the omelette under a pre-heated hot grill, and cook for 2–3 minutes until golden.
5 Slide on to a warm plate and serve in portions.

Serves 1–2.

◀ APPLE CAKE ▶

This cake uses Bramley apples which are grown commercially only in Britain.

75 g butter *or* margarine
175 g SR flour
75 g soft, light brown sugar
700 g Bramley cooking apples
grated rind of an orange (optional)
1 large egg

1 Set the oven at 190°C/375°F/Gas 5. Grease a 20 cm round cake tin or small roasting tin.
2 Sieve the flour into a bowl, cut the butter into pieces, and rub it into the flour using your fingertips. Add the sugar.
3 Peel, core, and dice the apple. Mix the apple and orange rind into the flour.
4 Beat the egg and mix in to make a stiff dough.
5 Pile into the tin and bake for 40–45 minutes until firm and golden brown. Serve hot or cold.

SCANDINAVIA

ICELAND
Reykjavik

LAPLAND

North Sea

SWEDEN

NORWAY

FINLAND

Oslo

Helsinki

Stockholm

DENMARK
Copenhagen

Baltic Sea

Scandinavia includes Norway, Sweden, Finland, Denmark, and, 600 miles to the west, the island of Iceland. Northern Scandinavian countries have long, dark, cold winters and short, warm summers, the only time when crops can be grown. The jagged coasts are dotted with islands and inland waterways and all five countries have large fishing fleets. Herring is caught in the Baltic Sea and cod and shellfish in the North Sea.

In the past much food needed to be preserved to last through the hard winters. The Vikings, sea raiders who came from Scandinavia in the eighth to tenth centuries, may well have been driven to explore other countries in a desperate search for food.

EATING IN SCANDINAVIAN COUNTRIES

Scandinavian countries have similar climates and foods, but each country has its own style of cooking.

FINLAND

Finnish cooking is based on simple wholesome foods. Hot soups, stews, potatoes, and porridges make warming winter dishes. The short summer is a time for gathering wild berries – raspberries, blueberries, and cranberries – and some of the 500 species of fungus that grow in Finland.

The Finns drink large quantities of milk and are fond of yoghurt and cheese. Bakers cook a wide range of breads made from wholewheat, rye, or barley flour.

DENMARK

Denmark is the most southerly of the Scandinavian countries. It has a climate similar to that of Britain. Since the Middle Ages Denmark has been known as a farming and seafaring nation. It is famous for its dairy foods: butter, cream, and cheeses, as well as for its ham and bacon. The Danish diet is the richest in Scandinavia.

SWEDEN

Nearly half of Sweden is covered in forest and woodland, and in the north, winter may last for more than six months. Swedish cooking is more adventurous than Norwegian but not as rich as Danish food. As in other Scandinavian countries, fish, especially herring, is popular, and so are dairy products.

ICELAND

Iceland is a treeless, rather barren land, and the country relies upon fishing as its main industry. Most food has to be imported.

LAPLAND

Lapland, running across northern Scandinavia, is snowbound for much of the year. Herds of reindeer provide both meat and milk for the Lapps. Reindeer meat, smoked and fresh, is popular throughout Scandinavia.

NORWAY

Norway has 3500 kilometres of coastline, and fishing is the country's most important industry. Norway is famous for its salmon, cod, and herring, exporting them all over the world.

Mountains and lakes make Norway difficult to cultivate, and much food is imported. Norwegians prefer good plain food and seldom use sauces, herbs, or spices. Plenty of dairy foods and fish, especially cod, are eaten.

Fishing boats in Bergen harbour

SCANDINAVIAN FOODS

THE SWEDISH SMÖRGÅSBORD

The smörgåsbord is famous all over the world and is popular in Sweden in restaurants and for parties. The smörgåsbord is like a buffet meal with a large spread of dishes, including hot food and a dessert. The idea is to make several trips to the buffet, helping yourself to small portions. Start with the herring dishes and then move on to eggs, shrimps, cold meats, salads, and cheeses. Finally try the hot food such as Jansson's Temptation, then a pudding and some coffee.

RYE

Nomadic tribes brought cereal grains across to Europe from the Middle East thousands of years ago. When wheat was planted, rye often grew as well and became a nuisance at harvest time. As people settled in northern lands, they found that rye thrived on poorer soils and in colder climates where other cereals would not grow.

Scandinavian rye crispbreads are popular in many countries as a substitute for bread and in low-calorie diets. Rye is similar in composition to wheat, but rye bread is slightly darker than the wheat loaf.

BRINGING HOME THE BACON

In Denmark, pigs were slaughtered in the autumn to save winter fodder. The meat was preserved by heavy salting, but the Danes were not very keen on this salted food and in the 1850s they began to sell it to Britain. Today Britain buys nearly half the bacon produced in Denmark, more than any other country!

DANISH SANDWICHES – SMØRREBRØD

Smørrebrød actually means 'buttered bread'. It may come from the days when rounds of bread were used as plates, then eaten at the end of the meal.

Each smørrebrød is a little meal in itself. The Danes use rye bread for the base, but small slices of white or wholemeal bread will do instead. The bread is well buttered to stop the topping from making the bread soggy. The cook then designs a topping made from any selection of meat, fish, cheese, and vegetables. Several kinds of smørrebrød are served together on a wooden platter, and you help yourself to one at a time, eating them with a knife and fork.

This display of smørrebrød includes toppings made from salami, paté, ham, sardines, eggs, and cheese.

14

THE HERRING

The herring is one of Europe's oldest foods –
herring bones were found in the rubbish from a
Stone Age Danish kitchen.

Scandinavians eat herrings in one form or
another almost every day. The smoked and salt
herrings date back to Viking times when they
were a valuable winter food store. Salt herrings
are preserved in wooden casks between layers of
rock salt, and are sliced for Danish sandwiches
and cold meals. The Finns make a rich herring
soup thickened with potatoes and cream.

The herring is a valuable food – one fish
provides a high proportion of a person's daily
nutritional needs. As well as protein and
minerals, the flesh contains oil, rich in vitamins
A and D.

DID YOU KNOW?

Cheese was valued as a type of currency
in the sixteenth century in Sweden. In
areas where pasture was owned by the
church, the local vicar took his rent in
the form of milk and fresh cheese. A
Swedish cheese called Prastost, meaning
parsonage cheese, is a reminder of this
old custom.

No one seems to know who Jansson really was,
but he invented the most delicious supper dish
made from anchovies and potatoes. Swedish
anchovies are small pickled herrings.

1 small can (about 50 g) anchovies (Scandinavian
are best)
4 large potatoes
1 large onion, finely chopped
25 g butter
200 ml milk
pepper

▼

1 Set the oven at 180°C/350°F/Gas 4.
2 Peel and slice the potatoes into thin chip
strips, then tip them into a bowl of cold
water.
3 Using some of the butter, grease a casserole
dish. Dry the potatoes in a clean tea-towel
and arrange some at the bottom of the dish.
4 Open and drain the anchovies. Lay some on
the potato, then sprinkle some onion over this.
Continue with layers of potatoes, anchovies,
and onions, ending with a potato layer.
5 Pour the milk over this. Sprinkle with pepper,
then dot with the rest of the butter.
6 Bake for 45 minutes until the potatoes are
tender. Serve hot.

Serves 2–3.

◀ RED CABBAGE ▶

Scandinavians are fond of red cabbage, serving it hot as a winter vegetable or pickled for use in summer with cold meats.

½ medium red cabbage
1 cooking apple
3 tbs white wine vinegar
6 tbs water
2 tbs blackcurrant juice *or* jam
salt
25 g granulated sugar

▼

1 Wash the cabbage and remove any old outer leaves. Lay it flat on a chopping board and slice finely. Peel and slice the apple.
2 Boil the vinegar and water in a large pan, then add the cabbage and apple. Cover and cook gently for 30 minutes, adding more water if the pan looks dry.
3 Add the sugar, salt, and juice or jam, and stir. This dish may be cooked for longer in the oven.

Serves 2–4.

◀ FRIKADELLER ▶

These meat balls are Denmark's national dish. Recipes vary – this one uses pork, but beef or veal can be used instead.

500 g finely minced pork
1 medium onion, finely chopped or grated
1 level tsp salt and some black pepper
1 beaten egg
3 level tbs SR flour
150 ml water
4 tbs vegetable oil for frying

▼

1 Using your hands, mix together all the meatball ingredients.
2 Heat the oil in a heavy frying pan. Using a tablespoon, shape the mixture into oval balls and place them in the pan. Fry for 6 minutes on each side. Continue until all the meat has been used up.
3 Serve hot with boiled potatoes, beetroot, or red cabbage, or cold for open sandwiches.

Serves 4.

SUGAR-BROWNED
◀ POTATOES ▶

These delicious potatoes are served as a Christmas treat.

about 20 small potatoes (*or* a large can)
25 g granulated sugar
25 g butter

▼

1 Scrub and boil the potatoes in their skins for about 20 minutes. Drain, cool, and peel off the skins. (*Or* open the can.) Rinse in cold water.
2 Melt the butter in a large heavy pan and as the butter begins to brown, add the sugar and stir. Take care not to burn yourself or the sugar!
3 Add as many potatoes as possible and shake the pan to roll and coat the potatoes. After about 10 minutes, place the hot potatoes on a warmed plate. Repeat until all the potatoes are used.

Serves 4.

WHIPPED BERRY
◀ PUDDING ▶

Scandinavians pick wild summer berries for this whipped creamy pudding.

1 medium can (about 400 g) of raspberries, strawberries, or redcurrants
or 600 ml sweetened, cooked red fruit
100 g semolina

▼

1 Purée the fruit and juice in a liquidizer or food processor. Make up to 600 ml with water.
2 Tip the purée into a large saucepan and bring to the boil, then sprinkle over the semolina. Stir with a wooden spoon and cook gently for about 10 minutes until the mixture thickens.
3 Pour this mixture into a mixing bowl. Using an electric whisk, beat the mixture at high speed for 10 minutes. (You can use a hand beater but it is hard work!)
4 The mixture becomes light and foamy and pale pink. Spoon into dishes and serve within a few hours.

Serves 4.

FRANCE

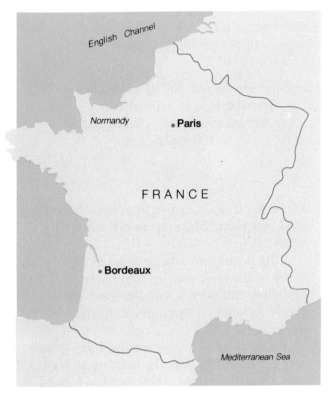

Charcuterie

France is the largest country in Western Europe and has a population of 54 million. It is a rich agricultural country which grows enough food to be virtually self-supporting. Crops include cereals such as wheat and barley, sugar, and fruit, especially apples, peaches, and grapes. Many animals are reared for meat, including goats and horses. Milk and milk products, especially butter and cheese, are widely used. France produces and exports many of the world's finest wines.

The French care very much about food. They choose the freshest, best quality ingredients and often cook them quite simply. Fresh bread is bought daily from the 'boulangerie' (baker's shop). The most popular type of loaf is the long, thin 'baguette' which is eaten with most meals. The 'boucherie-charcuterie' is a special butcher's shop selling raw meat and also pies, sausages, and pâtés, often made by the butcher. Street markets are found throughout France and shoppers inspect fruit and vegetables carefully before buying. Market stalls sell fresh herbs such as chives, parsley, and thyme for cooking.

FRENCH MEALS

Mealtimes are an important part of French life. Good food is carefully prepared and meals are not hurried.

Breakfast is a simple meal of bread, butter, jam, and coffee. Lunch is the main meal of the day, except when families work a long way from home; then the main meal is in the evening. Lunch might consist of pâté, followed by meat and vegetables, then salad, then a selection of cheeses, and finally fruit or sometimes dessert.

The evening meal is usually smaller, consisting, for example, of soup, an omelette, salads, cheese, and fruit.

SOME UNUSUAL FRENCH FOODS

ARTICHOKES

Globe artichokes are like giant thistle flowers. The artichoke is boiled for 25 minutes, then the hairy centre of the artichoke is removed. To eat an artichoke, pull out the leaves, dip them in a sauce, and suck the thicker end. After the leaves, the base or heart is eaten.

CHICORY

France is the largest producer of chicory in Europe. Good chicory should be crisp with white stems and yellow tips. It tastes slightly bitter and is used fresh in salads or cooked as a vegetable.

FROGS' LEGS AND SNAILS

Frogs' legs are a great delicacy in France and so popular that the French have to import them. They are fried in butter and served with a sauce. Frogs' legs are said to taste like tender chicken.

Snails in France are often bred on snail farms. Snails need careful cleaning. They are boiled for nearly an hour, then served in their shells with garlic butter, or made into other dishes.

Buying cheese in Rouen indoor market

FRENCH CHEESES

France makes over 365 varieties of cheese – more than any other country in the world. The French have made cheese for two thousand years using milk from cows, sheep, and goats. Famous cheeses include Camembert, Brie, Roquefort, and Saint Paulin. Some creamy cheeses are flavoured with garlic, herbs, and spices.

In France a selection of cheeses is served after the main course of a meal and before the fruit or dessert. French people are the world's greatest cheese eaters. In 1979 each person ate over 17 kg of cheese.

GARLIC

The best garlic in the world is grown in the South of France and garlic has long been associated with French cooking. Garlic probably came from Central Asia and is one of the oldest foods in recorded history, mentioned both in the Bible and in ancient Egyptian writings.

TO PREPARE GARLIC

Garlic bulbs are made up of cloves enclosed in a white paper-like skin. Choose a firm bulb, break off a clove, peel off the skin, and remove any dry root. Chop the garlic on a board, sprinkle with salt, then using the flat edge of the knife, smash the pieces into a paste. Large chunks of garlic can be unpleasant to eat.

GROW YOUR OWN GARLIC

Garlic grows in many climates. In the winter or early spring plant some cloves, root end downwards, about 4 cm deep in soil. The garlic bulb will be ready to harvest in June or July. A large crop may be plaited together, using the leaves.

◄ GARLIC BREAD ►

1 loaf of French bread
100 g butter
2–4 cloves of garlic, peeled and crushed
salt
2 tbs chopped parsley

1 Set the oven at 200°C/400°F/Gas 6.
2 Cut the loaf into 4 cm slices, almost through to the bottom crust.
3 Beat together the other ingredients to make the garlic butter and spread the mixture between the slices of bread.
4 Wrap the loaf in foil and bake for 15–20 minutes. Serve hot.

DID YOU KNOW?

Garlic was the cause of the first strike in history. Slaves stopped work on the Pyramids in Egypt because their garlic ration was cut.

This soup is popular in Northern France where the onions grow. It is served topped with crunchy bread and cheese.

> 4 large onions, peeled and sliced into rings
> 2 tbs vegetable oil *or* 50 g butter
> 1 level tbs flour
> 1 litre of water
> 1 beef stock cube
> 4 slices of French, or thick, bread
> 50 g grated cheese

1 Heat the oil *or* butter in a large pan, and fry the onions until they turn golden brown. This may take 15–20 minutes.
2 Sprinkle in the flour and cook for 1 minute, stirring with a wooden spoon. Add the water and stock cube. Boil, cover, and simmer for 20 minutes.
3 Set the oven to 190°C/375°F/Gas 5. Place the bread on a baking tray, sprinkle with cheese, and bake in the oven for 10 minutes until the cheese melts *or* use the grill.
4 Pour the soup into bowls and float the cheesey bread on top.

Serves 4.

Serve this coarse pâté with salad and French bread.

> 225 g minced pork
> 225 g chicken livers
> 1 small onion, finely chopped
> 1 clove of garlic, peeled and crushed
> salt and plenty of black pepper
> 1 tsp dried thyme
> 1 tbs chopped parsley, fresh or dried
> 6 rashers of streaky bacon
> 1 bay-leaf

1 Set the oven at 200°C/400°F/Gas 6.
2 Remove the rind from the bacon. Stretch the bacon, using the back of a knife. Line a medium loaf tin or dish with the bay-leaf and bacon.
3 Finely chop the chicken livers or blend in a liquidizer. Mix all the ingredients together and press into the tin, folding over any bacon rashers.
4 Cover with foil and stand the tin in water in a roasting tin. Cook for 45 minutes. Remove from the tin, pour off the juice, and leave to cool. When cool, wrap in foil. After a day the flavour improves.

Serves 4–6.

◄ SALADE NIÇOISE ►

This fish salad from the South of France may be served as a starter or as a main course with crusty bread.

2 eggs
4 firm tomatoes
½ onion, peeled and sliced
½ crisp lettuce (Iceberg or Webbs)
1 green pepper
200 g can of tuna fish
50 g frozen French beans
1 small can (about 50 g) of anchovy fillets
50 g black olives (optional)

French dressing
8 tbs vegetable oil
4 tbs wine vinegar
1 crushed clove of garlic
2 level tsp French mustard
½ level tsp each of salt, pepper, and castor sugar

▼

1 Boil the eggs in water for 8–10 minutes, then place in cold water to prevent a black ring forming round the yolk. Peel and cut into quarters.
2 Cook the beans as directed on the packet and leave to cool.
3 Wash, dry, and shred the lettuce. Wash the pepper, remove the core and seeds, and slice. Wash and quarter the tomatoes. Arrange these vegetables in a bowl.

4 Drain the juice from the cans of anchovies and tuna. Using a fork, flake the tuna flesh. Arrange the fish on the salad and decorate with the pepper, olives, and eggs.
5 **Prepare the French dressing:** Put all the ingredients in a jam jar and screw the lid on. Shake vigorously just before serving to mix together the oil and vinegar. They will separate out if the dressing is left to stand.
6 Sprinkle some French dressing over the salad and serve immediately.

Serves 4–6.

◀ RATATOUILLE ▶

Ratatouille is made from the vegetables which grow in the Mediterranean area. It is delicious hot or cold, on its own or as a vegetable dish.

1 large onion, peeled and sliced
1 clove of garlic, peeled and crushed
2 tbs vegetable oil
1 small aubergine, washed and sliced
1 large green pepper, cored, deseeded and sliced
4 courgettes, washed and sliced
1 medium can (about 400 g) of tomatoes
salt and black pepper

1 Heat the oil in a large pan and fry the onion and garlic until soft.
2 Add the sliced aubergines and fry for a further five minutes.
3 Stir in the remaining ingredients, then simmer the mixture, half covered, for 30 minutes.
4 The ratatouille is ready when the vegetables are soft but still in shape and most of the liquid has evaporated.
5 Serve hot or cold.

Serves 4–6.

◀ CASSOULET ▶

Traditional ingredients for this bean and meat stew include goose, lamb, and pork, but this is a cheaper version!

2 onions, peeled and sliced
1 clove of garlic, peeled and crushed
200 g well flavoured pork sausages, halved
1 breast of lamb with most fat removed
1 medium can (about 425 g) each of haricot and butter beans
1 small can (about 200 g) of tomatoes
200 g smoked garlic sausage, cut into chunks
salt and pepper
1 beef stock cube

1 Set the oven to 200°C/400°F/Gas 6.
2 Cut the lamb into 6–8 chunks and roast with the sausage in a tin for 20 minutes.
3 Fry the onion and garlic in the oil for 10 minutes until golden brown.
4 Drain the beans and tomatoes. Make up their juice to 400 ml with water and add the stock cube.
5 Mix all the ingredients together carefully in a casserole dish. Pour the tomato stock over the other ingredients and cover. Turn the oven to 180°C/350°F/Gas 4 and cook the casserole for 1½ hours until the meat is tender.

Serves 4.

◀ FRENCH APPLE TART ▶

Normandy is a region famous for its apple orchards.

Pastry
125 g plain flour
60 g butter
50 g castor sugar
1 egg yolk

3 large dessert apples (Cox's are best)
3 red-skinned dessert apples
2 tbs apricot jam

1 Sieve the flour into a bowl. Cut the butter into small pieces, then rub it into the flour using your fingertips. Add the sugar, then mix in the yolk and with your hands make a stiff dough, adding water if necessary. Wrap in foil or cling-film and leave in the fridge for half an hour.

2 Peel, core, and quarter the 3 apples. Cook in a covered pan with 3 tbs water for 5 minutes until the apple softens.

3 Set the oven to 200°C/400°F/Gas 6.

4 Roll out the pastry on a floured surface and use it to line a 20 cm flan ring or dish. The pastry is crumbly and even the best chefs have to patch it sometimes! Trim the edges and prick the bottom.

5 Spread the cooled cooked apple over the pastry. Cut the red apples into quarters, core and slice finely. Arrange a circle of overlapping slices around the flan. Spread one tablespoon of apricot jam over the top and bake for 30 minutes. Spread the remaining jam over the top and serve hot or cold.

Serves 4–6.

◀ CHOCOLATE MOUSSE ▶

This popular French dessert is very rich, so serve only small portions.

200 g plain chocolate
4 eggs

1 Put the chocolate in a large bowl. Place this over a pan of simmering water until the chocolate has melted. Do not get water into the chocolate.
2 Make sure bowls and utensils are clean before separating the eggs. Use a separate bowl for each egg in case the yolk breaks. Make a firm crack in the middle of the egg using a knife. Hold the egg over a bowl and remove the shell top, letting some white slip out into the bowl. Tip the yolk onto your hand and the remaining white will slip out. Put the yolks all together, and the whites in a separate large bowl.
3 Using an electric or rotary whisk, beat the egg whites until stiff but not dry.
4 With a metal spoon, stir the yolks in to the chocolate. Mix in a third of the egg white and then gently fold in the remaining white. Try to avoid flattening the mixture.
5 Spoon into a serving dish and chill

Serves 2–4.

DID YOU KNOW?

The French invented **margarine**. In 1869 the food chemist of Napoleon III invented a cheap substitute for butter. He mixed together suet, chopped cow's udder, and milk, and made a pale waxy fat. He called this margarine after the Greek word for pearl, 'margaron'.

SPAIN AND PORTUGAL

Bay of Biscay

PORTUGAL S P A I N

• Madrid

Valencia • Mediterranean Sea

Lisbon •

Balearic Islands

Spain and Portugal share the area of south-west Europe known as the Iberian peninsula. The north with its heavier rainfall is good for crops and grazing land, but the dry plains of central Spain are difficult to cultivate. In the hot south many types of fruit are grown, especially grapes which are made into wine and sherry.

In both countries cooking is simple, using plenty of vegetables, especially tomatoes, onions, peppers, and olives. Since the area is surrounded by sea, there are many varieties of fish. The Portuguese are famous for their sardines and also enjoy dried salt cod fish which they cook in different ways. Little milk or cheese is eaten and olive oil is often used instead of butter.

Fruits such as oranges, figs, pomegranates, and grapes are eaten instead of puddings. This may be why Spain and Portugal use half the amount of sugar eaten in the UK or the USA.

HISTORY

Spain and Portugal used to consist of several separate kingdoms but in 1143 Portugal became an independent country. Between the sixth and thirteenth centuries the Moorish tribes from north Africa occupied the area. They planted groves of oranges, lemons, and almonds, and laid down carefully irrigated fields of rice, now one of Spain's staple foods. The Moors brought with them exotic spices from the East, flavours still used in food today.

Spanish explorers of the New World brought home tomatoes, peppers, and chocolate, which the Spanish soon learned to enjoy.

A lemon grove

SPANISH MEALS

The Spanish like to eat crusty bread with all their meals. Main meals are often served with wine and bottled spring water.

An early breakfast of milky coffee and rolls is followed by a late lunch at around 2 p.m. This might consist of soup, then a bean and meat stew, followed by fresh fruit and coffee. In the heat of the afternoon the Spanish rest inside, taking their famous 'siesta'.

The evening meal is taken much later, often after 9 p.m. This is a lighter meal of meat, potatoes, and salad, then fruit and coffee.

Before the evening meal the Spanish may go to a bar to eat **tapas**. These are tasty snacks such as stuffed eggs, olives, or sausages. The name 'tapa' means 'lid'. The story goes that a barman once covered his customer's drink with a slice of bread to keep out the flies, and so created the first tapa.

OLIVES

With 200 million olive trees, Spain is the world's largest exporter of olive oil. When the fruit ripens from green to black, the trees are beaten and the ripe fruit falls into nets. The olives are pressed and the oil is squeezed out. Olive oil is used for salad dressings and for cooking. The Spanish dip their bread in it.

Whole green or black olives are eaten after pickling in salt solution.

PAELLA

Valencia on the east coast of Spain is the home of paella. This is a dish made from different foods grown in the area. Rice, saffron, and various seafoods, plus tomatoes and peas, are all cooked together in a pan called a **paelleria**. The cook can add any other food of his or her choice. The original dish was made from snails, eels, and green beans.

DID YOU KNOW?

Tomato ketchup was invented by the Spanish.

The court chef mixed together wild tomatoes which explorers had brought back from Peru, with oil, vinegar, onions, and pepper.

◄ TORTILLA ESPAGNOLA ►

Tortilla is the Spanish word for omelette. It looks like a flat round cake and traditionally contains only eggs, potatoes, and onions, although other foods can be added.

2 large potatoes, peeled and sliced
1 medium onion, peeled and sliced
3 eggs
salt and pepper
a little oil for frying

1 Heat the oil in a medium omelette or frying pan, then add the potatoes and onions. Fry gently and stir, then cover with a lid and cook gently for 15 minutes.
2 Beat the eggs with some salt and pepper in a large bowl. Remove the pan from the heat and lift out the vegetables, mixing them into the eggs.
3 Wipe out the pan with a paper towel to remove any bits. Add a little more oil. Pour in the egg mixture and cook for 5 minutes until it sets. Turn on the grill, then place the pan underneath, taking care not to burn the handle.
4 Cook until the tortilla is golden brown. Turn on to a plate and cut into wedges. Serve hot or cold.

Serves 2–4.

◄ GAZPACHO ►

This famous cold Spanish soup was first made by pounding together any suitable salad vegetables that were available. Serve it very cold with chopped parsley and olives.

6 chopped tomatoes *or* 1 medium can
(about 400 g) of tomatoes
½ cucumber, roughly chopped
1 green pepper, cored, deseeded, and chopped
1 slice of bread with crusts removed
1 crushed clove of garlic
1 tbs white wine vinegar
1 tbs olive oil
salt and pepper

1 Crumble the bread, then soak it in the oil, garlic, and vinegar.
2 Purée the bread and vegetables in batches in a blender or food processor.
3 Pour into a serving bowl and stir in 150 ml ice cold water. Season well and chill.

Serves 4–6.

Note: The vegetables may be finely chopped instead of blending.

◄ COCIDO MADRILENO ►

Country people prepare one-pot stews called **cocidos** from any meats or vegetables to hand. This one is the most famous.

100 g dried chick-peas soaked overnight (*or* a medium can (about 430 g) of chick-peas)
2 rashers smoked bacon, chopped
100 g fine garlic salami or Spanish chorizo
250 g stewing pork, finely sliced
2 carrots, peeled and chopped
2 potatoes, peeled and chopped
2 onions, peeled and sliced
salt and pepper

1 Cut the sausage into small chunks.
2 Half fill a large saucepan with water and add the sausage, bacon, meat, and chick-peas. Boil, then skim off any frothy scum. Simmer for half an hour, then add the vegetables. Cook for another hour, then season well. When the meat and chick-peas are tender the cocido is ready.
3 Traditionally the broth is served first, then the vegetables and meat.

Serves 2–4.

◄ ALMOND CAKES ►

The flavour of almonds in these little cakes is a reminder of the Moors who planted the almond groves centuries ago.

100 g plain flour
100 g castor sugar
75 g ground almonds
1 beaten egg
almond essence
1 tbs milk
a few flaked almonds

1 Set the oven at 140°C/275°F/Gas 1.
2 Mix the flour, sugar, and ground almonds in a bowl. Pour in the egg and a little almond essence. Use a fork to form a dough. Soften with milk if necessary.
3 Shape teaspoonfuls of the mixture into balls, then brush with milk and decorate with almonds. Place on a baking tray.
4 Bake for 30 minutes, then leave to cool.

ITALY

Caravaggio: The Young Bacchus

Italy is an easy country to remember – it looks like a boot jutting out into the Mediterranean with the toe kicking Sicily into the sea.

Being such a long, narrow country the climate changes from the snowy mountains in the extreme north, through the milder plains in the centre, to the hot dry lands of the south.

Rice and maize are grown in the north and there is good grazing land for cows and goats. These animals produce milk for butter and cheese as well as being used for meat. Olives grow in the warmer regions and are used for olive oil. Tomatoes and citrus fruits are grown in the south. Italy grows more of these fruits than any other European country.

Wheat is grown in the north, and in the southern state of Puglia on the 'heel' of Italy grows the hard durum wheat used in the production of pasta.

The surrounding seas provide a wonderful selection of exotic fresh fish, including sardines, tuna, anchovy, octopus, and squid.

The Italians are also proud to be the largest wine-producing country in Europe.

Italy has a long history of good cooking. The Romans brought back many exciting foods from their conquests. Roman banquets were famous.

The Italians even taught the French how to cook! When the Italian lady, Catherine of Medici, married the King of France, she took her Italian chefs with her. The French liked the new recipes and copied them.

Today Italy is still famous for its good food.

FOODS AND COOKING METHODS

Italian food varies from one part of the country to another. Each region concentrates on using its own local ingredients. Even pasta, which is eaten everywhere in Italy, is cooked in different ways with different sauces. Both olive oil and butter are used in cooking. Olive oil is more popular in southern Italy and butter is used in the north. Legend has it that butter was invented in Milan.

CHEESES

Italy produces many different cheeses. Two well-known ones are Parmesan and Mozzarella. **Parmesan** is a hard cheese still made from a 700-year-old recipe. It takes 16 kilograms of milk to make one kilogram of cheese and the cheese is matured for two years. Freshly grated Parmesan is sprinkled over pasta dishes and soups. **Mozzarella** was traditionally made from buffalo's milk but today cow's milk is sometimes used. Mozzarella is a soft white cheese used for pizzas, which when cooked pulls into strings like chewing gum.

FOODS FROM THE NEW WORLD

Explorers brought back many plants from their voyages. **Tomatoes** thrived in the Italian sunshine and cooks used them for pasta sauces and pizza toppings. Italian plum tomatoes are exported all over the world in cans and as tomato concentrate. **Maize** grew well in northern Italy. Local people make a dish from maize and water called 'polenta' which is served with stews or topped with butter and cheese.

ITALIAN ICE-CREAM

The Chinese probably invented ice-cream but the Italians perfected the recipe and made ice-cream popular all over the world. In the Middle Ages the Arabs taught the Italians the art of freezing fruit juices. In 1670 a Sicilian opened the first ice-cream parlour in Paris and six years later there were 250! Today the Italians are considered to be the best makers of ice-cream.

Manufacturing Parmesan cheese

Italian tomato products are a major export.

ITALIAN MEALS

A local Italian football team tuck into spaghetti.

Bread is eaten with most Italian meals. By eating both bread and pasta, Italians eat more cereals than any other Europeans.

Italians start the day with a light breakfast of coffee and some bread or rolls. This is followed by two main meals – one in the middle of the day, the other at eight or nine o'clock at night.

Traditionally Italian meals started with **antipasti**. This is a selection of titbits which might include thinly sliced smoked ham, spicy sausages, stuffed vegetables, and cold fish. Antipasti are usually served at special meals. For ordinary meals, the first course might be soup or some sort of pasta such as spaghetti or macaroni with a sauce and grated parmesan. In Italy pasta is not usually served as the main course. The rest of the meal might be a meat or fish dish with salad or one or two vegetables. Italians do not bother much with puddings and prefer to eat cheese and fresh fruit. However, sometimes delicious ice-creams are served, or a pudding called 'Zuppa Inglese' which is an Italian version of the English trifle.

Wine is often drunk with meals and a small coffee is served at the end. The Italians invented **expresso** coffee. Steam instead of water is forced through very finely ground coffee, making a very strong coffee indeed. A weaker version is served with sugar and a frothy milk topping. This is called **cappuccino**.

Cappuccino (top) and expresso (bottom)

DID YOU KNOW?

Did you know that the Italians introduced the table fork to Britain? In the seventeenth century an Englishman called Thomas Coryat travelled to Italy and brought home the table fork. The Italians had been using them for one hundred years!

◄ MINESTRONE SOUP ►

Minestrone is the most famous Italian soup. It contains so many nourishing ingredients that it is almost a meal in itself. In fact 'minestrone' means 'large soup'. The Italians use pinky-brown Borlotti beans in minestrone, but butter or broad beans can be used instead.

1 tbs vegetable oil
1 onion, peeled and diced
3 rashers of bacon, chopped
2 stalks of celery, washed and chopped
1 carrot, peeled and diced
1 small can (about 220 g) of butter or broad beans
50 g macaroni
1 chicken stock cube
pinch each of salt, pepper, and oregano
1 litre water
50 g green cabbage, finely shredded
50 g grated Parmesan or Cheddar cheese

1 Heat the oil in a large pan and fry the onion and bacon until they just turn brown. Add the carrot and celery and cook for a further two minutes.
2 Pour in the water and add the beans with their juice, the stock cube, salt, pepper, oregano, and macaroni. Cover with a lid, then bring to the boil and simmer for 10 minutes.
3 Add the cabbage to the soup and cook for a further five minutes until the macaroni is 'al dente': that is, chewy but not too soft.
4 Serve the soup hot, sprinkled with cheese and eaten with hunks of crusty bread.

Serves 4–6.

DID YOU KNOW?

In the eighteenth century groups of rich young Englishmen used to travel to Italy for long holidays. They so enjoyed the Italian pasta macaroni that they formed their own group called the Macaroni Club. They invented a dish called 'Macaroni cheese' to encourage others to try out the new taste.

◀ PASTA ▶

Pasta is made from finely-ground durum wheat which has been mixed with water to form a dough. Legend has it that the explorer Marco Polo stole the recipe from the Chinese and brought it back to Italy.

Pasta can be bought dried or fresh from supermarkets or Italian shops. There are over one hundred different shapes and sizes of pasta. Pasta comes in different colours too: eggs make the dough yellow and spinach turns it green. Wholewheat pasta is pale brown in colour.

The different types of dried pasta are made by pressing the dough into different shaped moulds to make shells, spirals, or wheels. The dough can be squeezed out to give solid or hollow lengths for vermicelli, spaghetti, or macaroni.

TO COOK PASTA

Allow 50–75 g of pasta per person: pasta will more than double its weight when cooked. Cook the pasta in a large saucepan of fast-boiling water for 10–15 minutes (longer for wholewheat pasta). The pasta should be cooked 'al dente'. This means 'to the tooth': in other words, not too soft, but chewy with some bite in it.

HOW TO MAKE YOUR OWN PASTA

100 g plain flour
pinch of salt
1 egg, beaten

1 Sieve the flour and salt into a bowl and add the beaten egg. Work into a dough, using a wooden spoon. Using your hands, squeeze the dough into a ball.
2 Knead the dough on a floured surface for 5–10 minutes. Cover with cling-film or foil and leave to rest for 30 minutes.
3 Flour the work top. Roll out the dough, pulling it into shape until it measures about 30 x 30 cm. Lift the dough occasionally.
4 This pasta can be cut into strips 1 cm x 30 cm for noodles, thicker strips for lasagne – 5 x 10 cm – or the whole sheet can be made into ravioli squares.
5 **Noodles:** Boil the noodles in water for 5–7 minutes. Drain and serve with butter, parsley, and grated Parmesan cheese.

◀ BAKED LASAGNE ▶

Lasagne is the flat wide pasta which is sometimes coloured green with spinach. This dish is made up with layers of pasta, meat sauce, and white sauce, then baked in the oven. The meat sauce can be served with other pastas such as spaghetti.

150 g dried lasagne
50 g grated Parmesan or strong cheese

Meat sauce
200 g minced beef
1 onion, peeled and chopped
1 carrot, peeled then grated
2 tbs tomato paste (*or* ketchup)
1 small can tomatoes, chopped
pinch each of salt, pepper, and oregano

White sauce
50 g margarine or butter
50 g flour
600 ml milk
salt and white pepper

1 Half fill a roasting tin with boiling water. Lay the dried lasagne in this and boil on the top of the stove for 10–15 minutes until the lasagne is 'al dente'. Drain and leave on a tea-towel until required. **NB**: Some lasagne is specially treated and does not need boiling before use (nor does homemade lasagne).

2 **Prepare the meat sauce**: Fry the mince in a large pan with the onion and carrot for 5–7 minutes, stirring occasionally. Add the tomato paste, chopped tomatoes and juice, salt, pepper, and oregano. Cover and simmer gently for 15 minutes.

3 **Now make the white sauce**: Place all the sauce ingredients in a small saucepan and heat, stirring all the time until the sauce thickens. Season to taste with salt and pepper.

4 Set the oven at 190°C/375°F/Gas 5.

5 **Assemble the lasagne**: Grease a large ovenproof dish. Arrange sheets of lasagne, meat sauce, and white sauce in layers, starting with the pasta and ending with the sauce.

6 Grate the cheese on top. Bake in the oven for 30 minutes until the top is golden brown. Serve with salad. *Serves 2–4.*

◀ HAM AND PEA RISOTTO ▶

Risotto is a creamy rice dish usually eaten as the first course of an Italian meal. Italy is the largest producer of rice in Europe. The sailors of Venice brought rice to Italy centuries ago and risotto rice now grows in the Po valley in northern Italy. Saffron is used to flavour and colour the rice but turmeric is a cheaper substitute.

2 tbs vegetable oil
1 onion, peeled and finely chopped
100 g risotto *or* long grain rice
pinch of saffron *or* turmeric
1 chicken stock cube
approx. 300 ml boiling water
50 g cooked ham, cut into strips
100 g frozen peas
black pepper
25 g grated Parmesan or Cheddar cheese

▼

1 Heat the oil in a large pan. Fry the onion until it softens and just begins to brown.
2 Add the rice and use a wooden spoon to stir and coat the rice with the oil. Cook for 1 minute.
3 Dissolve the stock cube and saffron or turmeric in the boiling water. Add a little stock to the rice and stir. As the rice absorbs the stock, add a little more. The Italians say the secret of a good risotto is never to let it cook alone!
4 After cooking for 15 minutes, stir in the ham and peas and cook for a further 5 minutes.
5 The finished risotto is a mass of yellow grains and should be served hot, sprinkled with grated cheese. *Serves 2.*

DID YOU KNOW?

Saffron is the most expensive spice in the world: 25 grams of saffron costs about £100! The spice is difficult to collect. The stigmas from the purple saffron crocus are collected and dried. It takes 250,000 stigmas from 76,000 flowers to make only 450 grams of saffron.

Saffron has been used for centuries to flavour food in India, the Middle East, Britain, and the Mediterranean countries. In the past saffron was also used as a yellow dye for clothes.

◀ NEAPOLITAN PIZZA ▶

The pizza started out as an ancient Roman breakfast food. The people of Naples invented the Neapolitan pizza using simple local ingredients such as tomatoes and cheese. Traditionally the pizza is cooked on the hot brick floor of the bread oven after the ashes have been swept away. The Italians do not often make pizzas at home.

This recipe is a simple basic recipe, but you can invent your own topping by adding other ingredients.

Dough
225 g strong bread flour (wholemeal or white)
150 ml warm water
30 g fresh yeast *or* 15 g dried yeast + 1 tsp sugar
½ tsp salt

Topping
1 tbs vegetable oil
1 medium can (about 400 g) of tomatoes
100 g strong grated cheese *or* Mozzarella cheese
pinch each of salt, pepper, and oregano

▶

1 **Dried yeast:** sprinkle the yeast and sugar into the warm water and leave to froth for about 10 minutes. **Fresh yeast:** crumble the yeast into the warm water and mix.
2 Sieve the flour and salt into a bowl and stir in the water and yeast. Mix until the dough forms a ball, adding more or less water as necessary.
3 Turn the dough on to a lightly floured surface. Knead and pull for 5–10 minutes.
4 Grease a large baking tray or shallow cake tin. Press the dough into a large circle and place on the tray. Set the oven at 220°C/425°F/ Gas 7. Leave the dough near the warm stove to rise.
5 Meanwhile prepare the topping. Chop the tomatoes in a bowl, then drain off most of the juice. Grate the cheese or slice the Mozzarella.
6 Brush the top of the pizza dough with oil. Spread the tomatoes over the dough and season well with salt, pepper, and oregano. Spread the cheese on top. Leave to rise for 20 minutes, then bake in the oven for 20 minutes or until the bottom of the pizza is firm. Cut into slices and serve hot or cold.

Serves 2–4.

CENTRAL EUROPE AND RUSSIA

Central Europe includes countries such as Austria, Germany, Hungary, Poland, and Czechoslavakia. For six hundred years much of this area was ruled by the Austro-Hungarian Empire and many of the countries have similar foods and ways of cooking.

Central Europeans enjoy their food. They serve nourishing soups and stews, often accompanied by dumplings, noodles, or potatoes. There are many varieties of breads made from wheat or rye flour. Cabbage of all kinds is one of the most popular vegetables since it is easily stored during the long winters.

GERMANY

Regional cooking in Germany still exists. Areas along the northern coastline enjoy fish, meat, and potatoes. In the south they prefer dumplings, pork, and sauerkraut, a salted cabbage. Germany produces an enormous selection of cheeses and the greatest variety of sausages in the world.

AUSTRIA AND HUNGARY

Dishes in Austria and Hungary are based on simple ingredients and are very filling. Austria is known for the Wiener Schnitzel, a thin slice of veal coated in breadcrumbs and cooked crisp and golden.

Hungarians make wonderful warming soups and stews, often flavoured with red paprika. Sour cream is used in many dishes and there is a saying that Hungarian food without sour cream is like life without love!

Both Austria and Hungary are famous for their cakes, pastries, and coffee shops. Apple Strudel with its crisp layers of light pastry, and Sacher Torte, a rich chocolate cake covered with apricot jam and chocolate icing, are well known and are popular at coffee time.

Coffee drinking in Austria is said to date back to the unsuccessful Turkish invasion in 1683. The Turks left behind some strange beans which an enterprising merchant recognized as coffee beans. He introduced the Austrians to coffee drinking and opened the first coffee house.

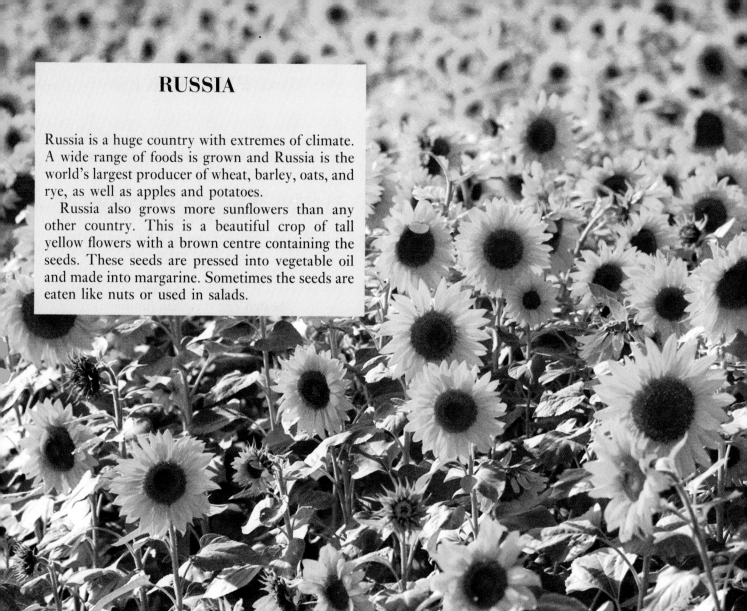

RUSSIA

Russia is a huge country with extremes of climate. A wide range of foods is grown and Russia is the world's largest producer of wheat, barley, oats, and rye, as well as apples and potatoes.

Russia also grows more sunflowers than any other country. This is a beautiful crop of tall yellow flowers with a brown centre containing the seeds. These seeds are pressed into vegetable oil and made into margarine. Sometimes the seeds are eaten like nuts or used in salads.

DID YOU KNOW?

How was the German **Pretzel** discovered? The story goes that a baker was thrown into prison for supplying bad bread. The authorities said they would free him if he could bake something that the sun could shine through three times. So he invented the three-holed pretzel!

SAUERKRAUT

Germans are fond of their salted cabbage, sauerkraut, and each person eats nearly 2 kg a year. White cabbage is chopped, placed in wooden barrels, salted, and left to ferment for several weeks.

Sauerkraut is usually sold in jars or cans and may be flavoured with juniper berries, cloves, or beer!

SAUSAGES

Central Europe is famous for its sausages. The wild boar has been found in the area since earliest times and many sausages are made from pork. Germany has over 1,500 different sausages and they are eaten for breakfast, snacks and main meals. By law, German sausages must contain 100% meat. **Wurst** is the German name for sausage and the different types of sausage include Bratwurst, Bockwurst, Frankfurters, and Knackwurst.

Poland has a large variety of sausages too and both Hungary and Poland are famous for salami made from pork or beef and flavoured with various spices.

DID YOU KNOW?

The frankfurter really did come from the city of Frankfurt. At one time only sausages made by the butchers of the 'Sausage Quarter' of Frankfurt could be called frankfurters. Today they are made elsewhere. Frankfurters are usually made from pork and are lightly smoked.

◀ PIROSHKI ▶

Piroshkis are little savoury pies from Russia which can be eaten with soup or as a snack.

1 packet (200 g) frozen puff pastry, defrosted
Filling
50 g mushrooms, washed but not peeled
50 g long grain rice
2 eggs
salt and pepper
beaten egg for glaze (optional)

1 Boil the rice and the eggs together in a pan for 10 minutes. Strain, then cool them.
2 Finely chop the mushrooms. Peel and chop the eggs. Mix all the filling ingredients together.
3 Set the oven at 220°C/425°F/Gas 7.
4 Roll out the pastry thinly on a floured surface. Using an 8 cm cutter or a glass, cut out circles of pastry. Reroll to use up scraps.
5 Put teaspoons of filling in the centre of each circle. Wet round the edges with water, using your finger or a brush. Fold the pastry over into a crescent and press round the edges to seal. Brush with beaten egg if you wish.
6 Place the crescents on a baking tray and cook for 15–20 minutes. Serve hot or cold.

◀ BORSCH ▶

For Russians, soup is an important part of the midday meal. This beetroot soup can be eaten hot or cold.

25 g butter *or* 1 tbs vegetable oil
2 very large raw beetroots
1 onion, peeled and finely chopped
1 litre of water
2 beef stock cubes
salt and pepper
chopped parsley or chives to garnish
2–3 tbs sour cream or natural yoghurt

1 Peel and grate the beetroot. Heat the butter or oil and fry the beetroot and onion for 5 minutes.
2 Add the water and the stock cubes. Bring to the boil, then cover and simmer for 30 minutes, stirring occasionally.
3 Serve hot or cold with a dollop of sour cream or yoghurt and a sprinkling of parsley.

Serves 4.

◀ 'HEAVEN AND EARTH' WITH FRANKFURTERS ▶

This German dish got its name because of the ingredients – the apples grow towards heaven and the potatoes down to earth! Potato and apple make a delicious accompaniment to any sausage or pork dish.

700 g potatoes, peeled and cubed
2 large cooking apples, peeled, cored, and sliced
1 tbs sugar
½ tsp salt
1 tsp vinegar
1 onion, peeled and sliced
100 g bacon, diced
4 long or 8 short frankfurter sausages

1 Put the potatoes, apples, sugar, salt, and vinegar in a large pan. Just cover with water, then bring to the boil and simmer for 15 minutes.
2 Fry the onion and bacon together until tender and browned. Keep warm.
3 Heat the frankfurters by leaving in a pan of hot water for 5 minutes.
4 Drain, then mash the potatoes and apples. Spoon on to the serving dish, top with the onion and bacon, and serve with the frankfurters.

Serves 2.

Goulash is a famous Hungarian soup or stew coloured red by the spice paprika. People in northern Europe are fond of dumplings which are dropped into soups and stews or even made into desserts. This goulash uses the cheaper meat, pork, instead of traditional beef.

400 g lean pork, cut into chunks
1 large onion, peeled and chopped
50 g butter *or* 2 tbs oil
3 tsp paprika
1 medium can (about 400 g) of tomatoes
300 ml water
1 stock cube
1 tsp each salt and pepper
chopped parsley
Dumplings
3 level tbs strong bread flour
1 large egg, beaten
pinch of salt

1 Heat the butter or oil in a large pan and fry the meat until golden. Add the onions, salt, pepper, paprika, tomatoes, water, and stock cube.
2 Boil, then cover and simmer for 1 hour until the meat is tender. Add more water if necessary. The goulash may be cooked in a casserole dish in the oven at 190°C/375°F/Gas 5 for the same time.
3 **Dumplings**: mix all the ingredients together. Drop small quantities from a teaspoon into the goulash and cook for 4 minutes. Serve the goulash hot, sprinkled with parsley.

Serves 4.

PAPRIKA

In Hungary, paprika is the favourite spice used to colour and flavour soups and stews. Paprika is the dried ground spice of the sweet red pepper which originally came from tropical America. Poor Hungarians used it as a medicine against malaria, but it soon became popular to liven up otherwise dull food. Paprika is usually mild and sweet but some varieties are hotter.

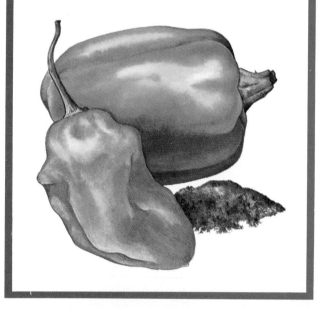

◀ HONEY CAKE ▶

This moist cake from Russia has travelled round the world with Russian Jews and is now the cake eaten at their New Year festival.

2 eggs
100 g castor sugar
6 tbs vegetable oil
4 tbs honey
150 ml warm water
350 g SR flour
½ tsp baking powder
½ tsp each of mixed spice and ground ginger
16 halved almonds

1 Set the oven at 190°C/375°F/Gas 5, and grease and flour two 20 cm round cake tins.
2 Warm the honey and oil in a bowl over a saucepan of hot water. Whisk the eggs and sugar until thick and creamy, then gently mix in the honey and oil.
3 Sieve the flour, baking powder, and spices into a bowl, then fold them into the egg mixture.
4 Stir in the water, then pour the mixture into the tins and decorate with the almonds. Bake for 40 minutes until the mixture is firm.

◀ MUESLI ▶

Today muesli is a popular breakfast dish which gives a filling and nutritious start to the day. Traditionally muesli came from Switzerland and a Swiss doctor invented his own recipe at the beginning of the century for patients in his hospital. Try making your own muesli using a recipe based on the Swiss idea.

2 dessert apples
2 tbs lemon juice
1 carton natural yoghurt (125 ml)
2 tbs honey
3 tbs water
100 g mixed cereal grains – oats, wheat, rye, millet
a few chopped nuts

1 Core and finely chop the apples, then toss in lemon juice.
2 Add the yoghurt, honey and water and stir in the cereal grains. Top with nuts.

Serves 2.

43

GREECE AND THE BALKANS

Fish have always been an important source of protein and the seas provide a great variety of fish and shellfish. Fish are cooked simply by grilling, frying, or baking in tomato sauce.

Countries around the Balkans include Greece, Yugoslavia, Bulgaria, and northern Turkey. The people are a mixture of races and the area has at different times been ruled by the Greeks, the Turks, and the Germans. The Turkish Empire introduced people to Middle Eastern foods and ways of cooking, and many of these dishes still remain.

The people of the area live on a simple diet very similar to that of the Ancient Greek civilization which began about 4000 BC. The Greeks ate barley bread, olive oil, vegetables such as peas, beans, cabbages, and lettuce, and fruits including grapes and figs.

In the south olives are eaten with most meals and olive oil is used in cooking. Further north sunflower oils and lard are used for cooking.

Through exploration and trade new fruit and vegetables have arrived and thrived in the area. These include aubergines, tomatoes, peppers, pumpkins, and melons.

Strong Turkish coffee is a popular drink. Sugar is added before the coffee is heated, so each person is asked how sweet they want their drink.

YOGHURT AND CHEESE

Yoghurt is widely eaten and used with salads, sauces, and as a dessert. Many people believe that it is the reason people here live so long and are so healthy. The very best yoghurt is said to come from Bulgaria which gave its name to the bacteria Lactobacillus Bulgaricus which is needed to change milk into yoghurt. True yoghurt is made from sheep's milk and is thick enough to cut with a knife. In Turkey they drink **ayran** made from yoghurt and iced water.

Cheese is another important source of protein. In Greece a soft, white sheep's or goat's milk cheese called **feta** is made.

SPECIAL FOODS

KEBABS

In this area lamb is the most popular meat. **Shish kebabs** are said to have been created by Turkish soldiers who stuck the lamb on their swords, then roasted it over an open fire. In Turkey, **doner kebab** is a boned leg of lamb roasted round a vertical spit. In restaurants, doner kebab is usually minced lamb pressed into a leg shape, then roasted.

SQUID AND OCTOPUS

At many Mediterranean fish markets squid and octopus are sold, and they are exported frozen. If you can buy one, look closely at the long tentacles and their suckers, and the head at the top of the body or 'bag'. Inside the 'bag' is a plastic-like 'backbone' and an ink sac which the animal squirts as a defence mechanism. Fishermen bash octopus on the rocks to make it tender to eat. Both the tentacles and the body are eaten.

SWEETS AND DESSERTS

Both the Greeks and the Turks love sweets and cakes. **Turkish delight** is sold in a range of colours from gold to pink, covered in icing sugar. Pastries are often made from **phyllo pastry** – a very thin flour and water pastry usually sold ready made. Popular cakes made from layers of pastry, honey, and nuts include **baklavas** and **kataifi**.

GREEK MEALS

Breakfast is usually a strong cup of coffee with bread and sometimes feta cheese or salami. Lunch is the main meal of the day. It may start with a small appetizer such as taramasalata and bread, followed by a meat and vegetable dish such as moussaka, then sometimes fruit or a milk pudding. The evening meal is simpler, with perhaps bread, salad, cheese, and fruit, or the family may go out to the local restaurant.

Carving doner kebab

Cakes made from pastry, honey, and nuts

DID YOU KNOW?

Do you know what 'lady's navels' and 'lady's fingers' are? They are both Turkish pastries. The first is a ball with a dimple in the middle and the second is rolled into finger shapes. 'Lady's fingers' is also the name for the vegetable, okra.

◀ TARAMASALATA ▶

Tarama is the salted roe of the grey mullet – tuna fish – or smoked cod's roe. The Greeks invented this fish-roe pâté to make the expensive roe go further.

125 g tarama (smoked cod's roe is most readily available – this can be bought fresh or canned)
4 large slices white bread without crusts
1 small onion, finely grated
1 clove of garlic, peeled and crushed
up to 250 ml olive or vegetable oil

▼

1 Remove the skin from fresh roe. Soak the bread in cold water for 2–3 minutes, then squeeze dry.
2 Using a food processor or liquidizer combine all the ingredients except the oil. Gradually add the oil to make a smooth paste. Use a potato masher if no machines are available.
3 Serve with hot pitta bread, lemon wedges, and olives.

Serves 4 as a dip.

◀ AVGOLEMONO SOUP ▶

In Greece lemons are plentiful. The juice is squeezed over fish, meat, and salads and it gives the flavour to this famous Greek soup, sometimes called egg and lemon soup.

1 litre of water + 2 good chicken stock cubes
(*or* some good chicken stock)
2 heaped tbs short grain pudding rice
2 eggs
juice of a large lemon
1 tbs chopped dried or fresh mint

▼

1 Boil the water, stock cubes, and rice in a large pan. Stir, then simmer for 15 minutes.
2 Beat the eggs and lemon juice together. Add a cup of the hot soup to the mixture and whisk.
3 Remove the soup from the heat and stir in the egg mixture. Serve decorated with mint.

Serves 4.

◀ GREEK SALAD ▶

Greek salad may be served on its own or with meals. The feta cheese used is made from sheep's or goat's milk and is soft, white, and slightly crumbly. If difficult to buy, substitute another cheese.

4 large tomatoes, cut into pieces not slices
1 green pepper, cored, deseeded, and sliced
½ cucumber, sliced
½ onion, roughly chopped
100 g feta cheese cut into cubes
10 black olives (optional)
small pieces of lettuce

Dressing:
4 tbs olive oil
juice of 1 lemon
1 tsp each of salt, pepper, and oregano

▽

1 Put the vegetables in a salad bowl.
2 Shake the dressing ingredients in a screw-topped jar. Pour over the salad and toss.
3 Arrange the olives and feta cheese on top.

Serves 2–4.

◀ SHISH KEBABS ▶

This famous Turkish dish is popular throughout the Middle East as well as in Greece. The kebabs can be served in the pocket of pitta bread or with rice and salad.

600 g lean lamb, cut into cubes
1 large onion

Marinade
4 tbs olive *or* vegetable oil
juice of one lemon
1 tsp each of salt, pepper, and ground allspice

4 pitta breads
4 tomatoes, sliced
1 onion, peeled and sliced
lettuce leaves, shredded finely
1 lemon, cut into wedges

▽

1 Mix the marinade ingredients in a large bowl. Add the lamb cubes and leave to soak for 30 minutes.
2 Cut the onion in quarters and peel off the 'leaves'. Turn the grill on to high.
3 Thread some lamb then onion alternately on to 4 skewers. Grill the lamb for 8–10 minutes turning from time to time until well browned on the outside and slightly pink inside.
4 Warm the pitta bread under the grill. Cut down one length and open the pocket. Fill with the lamb, tomato, lettuce, and onion, and squeeze in some lemon.

Serves 4.

◀ MOUSSAKA ▶

Moussaka is a dish of baked mince and aubergine covered with a creamy sauce. If aubergines are not too expensive then use more.

1 large aubergine with stalk removed, sliced
4 tbs olive or vegetable oil
500 g minced lamb or beef
1 large onion, peeled and chopped
1 tbs tomato purée
salt and pepper
150 ml water
1 beef stock cube
1 tsp oregano
25 g margarine
25 g plain flour
300 ml milk
1 egg, beaten

▼

1 Put the sliced aubergine in a colander, sprinkle with salt, and leave for 20 minutes so that the bitter juices drain away. Rinse and pat dry.

2 Heat the oil in a frying pan and fry the slices until pale brown. Drain with a slotted spoon.

3 Cook the onion and minced meat in a pan for 10 minutes, stirring occasionally. (The meat contains enough fat for frying.)

4 Stir in the salt, pepper, tomato purée, oregano, water, and stock cube. Boil, then cover and simmer for 20 minutes.

5 Make the sauce. Heat the margarine, milk, and flour in a small pan, stirring all the time. As it boils, the sauce thickens. Remove from the heat and beat in the egg. Season with salt and pepper.

6 Set the oven at 190°C/375°F/Gas 5.

7 Prepare the moussaka – spread the meat mixture at the bottom of an ovenproof dish and arrange the aubergine slices on top. Spoon the sauce over the moussaka and bake in the oven for 35–40 minutes until golden brown. (With more aubergines there can be layers of meat and aubergine.)

8 Serve hot with Greek salad.

Serves 2–4.

◄ STUFFED PEPPERS, TOMATOES, AND ONIONS ►

In Greek restaurants large trays of locally-grown stuffed vegetables are prepared for customers. These may be served on their own or as a vegetable dish.

2 large peppers (green or red)
2 large tomatoes (beef tomatoes are best)
2 medium onions
Stuffing
150 g minced beef
100 g long grain rice
pinch of salt and pepper
60 g currants *or* sultanas, chopped
a little fresh or dried mint

▼

1 **Prepare the vegetables**: Cut off the top of the tomatoes and keep to use as lids. Scoop out the pulp to use for the filling.
   Peel the onions and trim off the top and roots. Remove the lid from the pepper and throw away the seeds. (Keep the lid.)
2 **Prepare the filling**: Boil the rice in plenty of water in a large pan for 10 minutes. At the same time boil the onions, then add the peppers for 5 minutes. Drain the vegetables and rice.
3 Using a knife, loosen the centre part of the onion and scoop out the middle with a teaspoon. Chop this part of the onion finely.
4 Fry the mince and chopped onion in a pan for 10 minutes, stirring occasionally. Add the rice, tomato pulp, currants, and seasoning.
5 Set the oven at 190°C/375°F/Gas 5.
6 Stand the peppers, tomatoes, and onions in a roasting tin and fill with the stuffing. Replace the lids and cover with foil. Put any spare stuffing in a small dish. Cook the peppers and onions for 30 minutes and the tomatoes for 15 minutes. Remove the foil and brown for 10 more minutes. Spare stuffing can be cooked as well.
7 Serve the vegetables hot or cold.
Serves 2.

RICE PUDDING
◄ WITH CINNAMON ►

This creamy pudding with a hint of lemon is made in Cyprus.

1 litre of milk
100 g long grain rice
75 g sugar
grated rind of 1 washed lemon
$\frac{1}{2}$ tsp cinnamon

▼

Boil the rice and milk for 30 minutes. Add the sugar and rind. Serve rice sprinkled with cinnamon.
Serves 4.

THE MIDDLE EAST

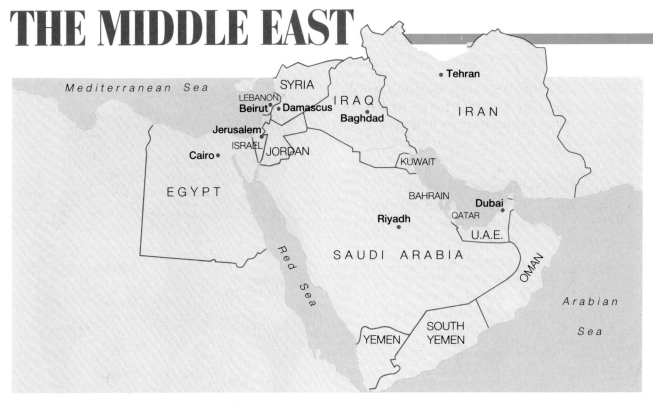

The Middle East is made up of fifteen countries in south-west Asia and north-east Africa, and has a population of over 100 million. People living in different parts of the Middle East lead very different lives. Many live in modern cities, some are nomadic Bedouin people living in the desert, and others farm fertile river areas.

Much of the land in the Middle East is desert with only 10 per cent under cultivation. The area is generally hot and dry with little rainfall.

Irrigation of the land to supply water to grow crops is essential throughout much of the region. The population is expanding and more food needs to be grown to avoid buying expensive imported food.

THE SPICE TRADE

For thousands of years the Middle East was the home of important spices and herbs. The ancient Egyptians used them for worship, magic, and medicine, and also as preservatives of food. For years the Arabs controlled the valuable spice trade, bringing rare spices from the orient and Asia Minor to the lands of the Mediterranean and the trading centres in Egypt.

Spices are used to flavour many Middle Eastern dishes. Favourites include cinnamon, cumin, allspice, and hot peppers. Fresh herbs such as coriander, mint, and parsley are sprinkled on food.

Sweet dishes may be scented with orange blossom or rose-water.

MIDDLE EASTERN FOODS

The basic Middle Eastern diet is a healthy one made up of cereals, especially wheat and rice, many varieties of beans, some meat, particularly lamb or goat, and fresh fruit and vegetables. With little pastureland there are few cows and so not many cow's milk products are used. Yoghurt may be made from sheep or goat's milk.

All kinds of fruit are grown including figs, dates, oranges, lemons, and grapes. Fruit is eaten dried or fresh. Vegetables include courgettes, aubergines, onions, and radishes. Chick-peas and lentils have been grown for thousands of years in the Middle East. Chick-peas make the dip **hummus** and rissoles called **falafel** which are sold in the streets.

Middle Eastern people are mostly **Muslims**, followers of the Islamic religion. Muslims must not eat pork and each year, during the month of **Ramadan**, thirty days are set aside for fasting. Muslims must not eat or drink between sunrise and sunset during Ramadan and at the end of the day there is a special meal. Muslims do not drink alcohol.

Wheat, the most popular cereal in the world today, came from the Middle East thousands of years ago. Wheat is probably the result of cross-breeding between two wild grasses since a wild wheat has never been found.

The Egyptians were the first people to grind wheat and make proper bread. Ancient Egyptians were called 'the bread eaters'; there were bakeries in Egypt in 2000 B.C.

Wheat is an important cereal in the Middle East. Bread is eaten with nearly every meal and small flat **pitta** bread is used to mop up foods, or it can be opened up and stuffed with salads, meats, or cheeses. **Shami** is the most common bread, coarser than pitta bread and made into rounds.

Burghul, known as **cracked wheat**, is whole wheat grains partially cooked then dried and cracked. Burghul is an essential ingredient in many soups, stews, and salads such as tabbouleh.

DID YOU KNOW?

The Egyptians were making sweets as early as 1600 B.C. They inscribed the method on tablets of stone.

Legend says that Arab herdsmen wandering the desert were the first to discover cheese. They carried ewe's milk in bags made from dried sheep's stomachs. The heat from the sun turned the milk sour and the sheep's stomach contained a little rennet which made a simple cheese. The oldest and most primitive cheese in the world is the Arabian **kishk**.

Harvesting wheat in ancient Egypt

FRUITS FROM THE MIDDLE EAST

POMEGRANATES

Pomegranates came originally from Persia, now Iran. Venus, the goddess of love, gave pomegranates as presents, and they have long been a symbol of fertility. The fruit has a hard red and yellow skin. Inside, the seeds are surrounded by soft pink jelly and may be eaten with a spoon or a pin. The fruit juice is usually made into refreshing drinks and into syrups.

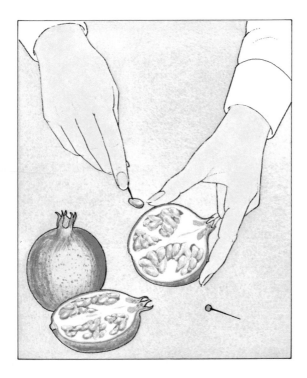

FIGS

The fig probably came from the Middle East and is one of the most ancient plants of civilization. Fresh figs can be white, green, purple, or black, depending on their variety. Because they have a tender skin they are difficult to export fresh, but they are sold canned and dried. Figs may be eaten with a fruit salad or baked in biscuits and cakes. Remember that figs act as a mild laxative, so don't overindulge!

DATES

The date palm has been cultivated in the Middle East since 3000 B.C. Today Iraq and Egypt produce over one third of the world crop of dates.

Date palms need plenty of water to grow and are found in oases in the desert where there is natural water. Areas around the River Nile in Egypt grow millions of dates.

The date palm is very tall, growing to 20 metres. It can bear fruit for sixty years. Each palm produces several clusters of dates, and each cluster can have as many as one thousand dates.

Dates are an important food in the Arab diet, especially for people living in desert areas. Dates contain 60–70 per cent sugar as well as vitamins A and B complex. Dates may be sold fresh, semi-dry in boxes, or they may be pressed into a lump.

Black figs

◄ DATE HALVA ►

This sweet from Iraq is quick to make and keeps well in a tin.

200 g stoned dates, finely chopped
50 g chopped walnuts
50 g chopped almonds
icing sugar

▼

1 Mix the dates and nuts together in a bowl, using your hands.
2 Dust a board with icing sugar then roll the date mixture into a sausage shape. Cut into rounds or squares and serve on a plate dusted with more sugar.

◄ YOGHURT ►

Yoghurt is made regularly in many Middle Eastern homes for eating on its own, mixing with other ingredients, and even making into a drink. Many Middle Eastern people believe that eating yoghurt leads to a long and healthy life.

MAKING YOGHURT AT HOME

600 ml UHT or Long Life milk (other milk needs boiling and cooling before use)
1 tbs freshly-bought natural yoghurt

1 Heat the milk to 43°C or until you can leave a clean finger in for just 10 seconds.
2 Add 1 tablespoon of yoghurt and mix well.
3 Pour into a clean, pre-warmed, wide-necked vacuum flask and close the flask. Leave undisturbed for 8–10 hours to allow the yoghurt to set.
4 Shake the flask and pour the yoghurt into a bowl. Cover and store in the fridge.

Another method is to pour the yoghurt and milk into a clean bowl, cover with a plate, and secure with elastic bands. Wrap the bowl in blankets and leave in a warm place for 8 hours.

◄ TABBOULEH ►

Tabbouleh is one of the national dishes of Syria and Lebanon. The **burghul** or cracked wheat is flavoured with vegetables and plenty of parsley, mint, and lemon.

75 g burghul (cracked wheat)
½ onion, finely chopped
½ cucumber, cut into very small cubes
3 tomatoes, finely chopped
4 tbs chopped parsley
a handful of fresh chopped mint
or 1 tbs dried mint
juice of 1½ lemons *or* 4 tbs lemon juice
4 tbs oil (olive oil tastes best)
salt and pepper
½ Cos lettuce *or* some good lettuce leaves

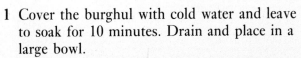

1 Cover the burghul with cold water and leave to soak for 10 minutes. Drain and place in a large bowl.
2 Mix in the onion, tomatoes, cucumber, parsley, and mint, and season well with salt and pepper.
3 Mix in the oil and lemon juice and leave to stand for 15 minutes.
4 Arrange the lettuce leaves on a dish and pile the tabbouleh on top. Serve on its own or with bread, hummus, and kebabs.

Serves 4.

◄ HUMMUS ►

Hummus is a thick creamy paste of chick-peas mixed with a crushed sesame seed paste called **tahina**. Hummus is usually served with pitta bread.

200 g chick-peas soaked overnight
or 1 medium can (about 430 g) of chick-peas
1 clove of garlic, peeled and crushed
2 level tbs tahina paste (sesame seed paste)
juice of 1 lemon *or* 3 tbs lemon juice
salt
1 tsp paprika

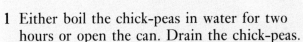

1 Either boil the chick-peas in water for two hours or open the can. Drain the chick-peas.
2 Keep a few chick-peas for decoration and purée the rest in a liquidizer or processor. Add the tahina, garlic, lemon juice, and salt, and beat well.
3 Spoon into a serving dish and decorate with chick-peas and a sprinkled line of paprika.

Serves 2–4.

CUCUMBER
◀ AND YOGHURT SALAD ▶

This cool mint-flavoured salad may be eaten on its own or with other dishes.

½ large cucumber, grated
1 clove of garlic, peeled and crushed
300 g natural yoghurt (2 small cartons)
1 tbs fresh chopped mint or dried mint
salt and pepper

▼

Mix all the ingredients thoroughly in a large bowl. Spoon into the serving dish and decorate with a sprig of mint.
Serves 4.

◀ KIBBEH ▶

Kibbeh is an ancient dish made in Syria and Lebanon. It is eaten with salad, pitta bread, hummus, and yoghurt. This recipe is baked in the oven, but kibbeh is often shaped and fried.

150 g burghul (cracked wheat)
300 g finely minced lamb *or* beef
1 large onion, finely grated or chopped
1 tsp ground allspice *or* cinnamon
salt and pepper
Filling
1 medium onion, finely chopped
150 g minced lamb *or* beef
½ tsp ground allspice
50 g chopped walnuts (optional)
50 g raisins, chopped

1 Set the oven at 200°C/400°F/Gas 6 and grease a baking tray or ovenproof dish.
2 Rinse the burghul in a sieve with cold water, then drain it and mix with the meat, onion, allspice, salt, and pepper. Either use the traditional method of pounding using a mortar and pestle, or blend to a paste in a processor.
3 For the filling, fry the onion and meat together until the meat browns. Add the allspice, nuts, and raisins.
4 Spread half of the first mixture on the bottom of the tray. Cover with the filling and top with the remaining mixture. Mark into diamond shapes with a knife.
5 Bake in the oven for 30–40 minutes until the top is well browned. Serve hot or cold with salad and yoghurt.

Serves 4–6.

◀ CHELO RICE ▶

In Iran different varieties of rice are grown and rice is cooked in several special ways. This steamed rice dish has a golden crust and a delicious flavour.

225 g long grain rice (Basmati is best)
250 ml water
50 g butter
1 tsp salt

1 Wash the rice in warm water three times, then leave to soak in water for 15 minutes. Drain the rice and rinse once more.
2 Boil the water and salt in a large pan. Add the rice and cover and cook for 10 minutes, stirring occasionally.
3 Strain the rice and rinse in warm water.
4 Melt 25 g butter and 2 tbs water in a pan. Gradually spoon in the rice and shape into a cone. Dot with the remaining butter.
5 Cover the pan with foil and two tea-towels, and then a lid. Cook gently for 30 minutes, then put the pan in cold water for a few minutes to loosen the crust.
6 A golden-brown crust forms on the bottom of the rice while the rest remains white. Serve with stews and dishes with sauces.

Serves 4.

◀ LAMB, APRICOT, AND PRUNE STEW ▶

Lamb is a very popular meat in the Middle East and this dish goes well with the rice.

500 g lean stewing lamb, cut into thin strips
1 large onion, finely chopped
2 tbs vegetable oil
1 tsp salt
$\frac{1}{4}$ tsp each of ground nutmeg, cinnamon, and pepper
juice of $\frac{1}{2}$ lemon *or* 2 tbs lemon juice
300 ml water
75 g dried apricots
75 g prunes

1 Soak the prunes and apricots in water.
2 Heat the oil in a large pan and fry the lamb and onion for 5 minutes, stirring with a wooden spoon. Add the salt and spices.
3 Pour in the water and lemon juice, then cover and simmer for 30 minutes or until the lamb is tender.
4 Drain the apricots and prunes and add to the meat. Simmer for 15 minutes. Serve with rice.

Serves 2–4.

◀ KHOSHAF ▶

During the month of Ramadan, Muslims fast all day and only eat after sunset. At the end of the day they enjoy dishes of beans, meatballs, kebabs, and this delicious dried fruit salad. If the salad is kept in the fridge for a few days the flavour improves.

100 g dried apricots
100 g prunes
100 g dried figs
50 g seedless raisins
50 g almonds or pinenuts

▼

1 Wash the fruit if necessary, then soak overnight.
2 Drain and put the fruit in a large pan. Cover with water and bring to the boil. Turn down the heat and simmer for 20 minutes.
3 Spoon into a serving dish and sprinkle over the nuts. Serve hot or cold.

Serves 4.

◀ MUHALLABIA ▶

Arab countries serve this rice pudding chilled, and flavour it with rose-water or sometimes orange blossom water. Chopped green pistachio nuts or almonds are used for decoration.

1 level tbs cornflour
50 g ground rice
600 ml milk
2 tbs rose-water *or* orange blossom water
50 g sugar
50 g ground almonds (optional)
chopped almonds to decorate

▼

1 Put the cornflour and rice in a large bowl and blend in 100 ml milk to make a smooth paste.
2 Boil the rest of the milk in a large saucepan. Using a wooden spoon, stir the milk into the rice paste.
3 Pour the mixture back into the pan. Heat and stir until the mixture boils and thickens. Add the rose-water and sugar and cook for a further minute.
4 Stir in the ground almonds if used and pour into serving dishes. Chill and decorate with nuts.

Serves 2–4.

AFRICA

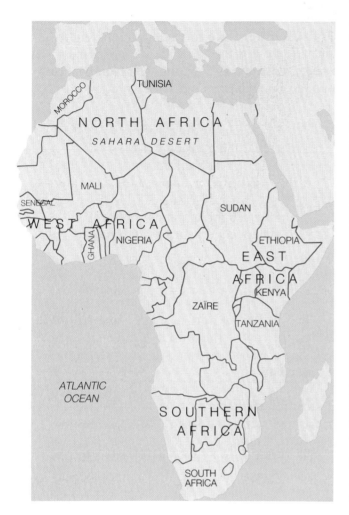

The vast continent of Africa covers 30 million square kilometres and is occupied by about 450 million people.

For centuries Africa has traded with, and been explored by, peoples from the Middle East, China, India, and Europe, and many ideas and foods have changed hands.

FOODS FROM AFRICA

Foods which grew wild in Africa have been taken to other parts of the world:
Coffee which came from Ethiopia is grown in South America, Indonesia, and the West Indies.
Sugar cane now grows in many tropical areas around the equator.

FOODS BROUGHT TO AFRICA

Selling maize in Kenya

Some plants from other countries grew well in Africa:
Cassava from America is a staple food in parts of West Africa.
Maize is an important crop in East Africa, and **wheat** in North Africa.
Many fruits which need constant warmth are grown in Africa. These include bananas, pawpaw, mangoes, grapes, citrus fruits, and peaches.

AFRICAN MEALS

A typical African meal is just one course, usually some sort of thick stew with meat or fish, and vegetables. This is served with some starchy food made from grains or roots. Chilli peppers are used to give many African dishes a spicy hotness. Fruit is eaten throughout the day at any time.

REGIONS OF AFRICA

NORTH AFRICA

The area north of the Sahara desert is known as North Africa and here the land is hot and dry with mountains and deserts. The people are descended from the ancient settlers, the Berbers, and from the Arabs who came as early as 1100 B.C. Farmers grow wheat, barley, beans, and chick-peas, and keep goats, sheep, and chickens. Fish caught from the surrounding seas include pilchards, anchovies, and red mullet.

EAST AFRICA

East Africa has areas with rich mineral deposits providing wealth. Maize is an important cereal throughout East Africa and is used to make a porridge called **ugali**, which may be eaten on its own or with meat, chicken, or vegetable stews. Large numbers of cattle as well as sheep and goats are reared in Kenya and Tanzania. Coffee and tea are valuable cash crops in several countries including Zaire and Kenya.

Oxen ploughing team, Kenya

WEST AFRICA

Market in Senegal

The important crops of West Africa include cassava, maize, and rice. Cassava is often made into a form of dumpling called **fufu**. Ghana is the world's chief cocoa-producing country, and other countries export cocoa as well as coffee and palm oil.

SOUTHERN AFRICA

South Africa, at the southern tip of Africa, is a country rich in minerals, with large cattle and sheep farms, and fertile areas growing crops of maize, sugar cane, and oranges.

Three hundred years ago, ships trading between Europe and the Far East in spices, silks, and ivory had to sail around the tip of Africa. Settlements were established on the Cape to provide fresh water, meat, and fruit and vegetables for the sailors.

The Dutch were among the first to arrive and eventually they settled, building homes and cultivating farmlands. People came from the Far East to work the land and help in the homes, introducing spicy dishes and new ways of cooking food. The Africans taught the settlers how to use millet to make porridge, bread, and beer.

Maize, introduced from South America, became the largest cereal crop. Corn-on-the-cob is known as **mielie**, and maize is made into mielie flour, porridge, and bread.

AFRICA'S FOOD PROBLEM

Drought in Mali

There are many reasons for Africa's present food problem. Over the past twenty years the population has increased rapidly. Since 1970 the production of food for local people has fallen steadily, and to make things even more difficult, large areas of Africa are prone to drought.

Traditionally in Africa crops have been grown and animals raised for local consumption. However, some farmers are keen to earn money by growing 'cash crops' which are usually sold for export. Valuable cash crops grown in Africa include palm oil, bananas, coffee, and cocoa. By using land for export crops, the soil becomes over used and there are also fewer crops grown for local use. During a major drought, these factors contribute to a severe food shortage.

In Africa south of the Sahara desert, one third of the children are undernourished, either because they do not get enough to eat or because they eat the wrong sort of food. Major causes of undernourishment include poverty, poor land, wars, and natural disasters.

There is no simple solution, but help is needed for irrigation schemes and land conservation to encourage farmers to produce more food for local people.

DID YOU KNOW?

In Nigeria cola nuts are offered to guests as a sign of welcome. They are chewed slowly to give a mild stimulating effect. The cola nut contains a little caffeine and is used as an ingredient in cola drinks.

Coffee originated in Ethiopia. According to legend a shepherd noticed that his goats started to leap about after eating the berries of a certain shrub. He tried the fruit himself and soon felt very happy. Local monks prepared a drink from the berries and used it to keep awake during prayers.

FOODS GROWN IN AFRICA

SORGHUM AND MILLET

The cereals sorghum and millet grow in the drier, less fertile regions of the world, and both crops are extremely important in Africa since they grow quickly in drought areas.

Sorghum is known as **Guinea corn** in West Africa and **kaffir corn** in Southern Africa. The grains may be used instead of rice, pounded into flour or made into beer.

Millet seed looks like large grains of sand and may be boiled like rice or made into flour for porridges.

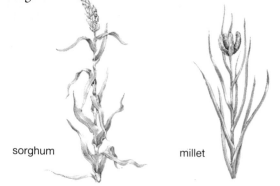

sorghum   millet

PALM OIL

The oil palm grows in Central and West Africa and a thick oily paste is made from the palm fruits. Palm oil is as important in Africa as olive oil is in the Mediterranean and butter is in colder countries. In Nigeria oil palms are often cultivated as cash crops. Palm oil is used to make margarine, cooking fats, and soap.

CASSAVA

The cassava plant was introduced into Africa from South America during the seventeeth century and now grows in tropical areas with plenty of rain. Cassava may be boiled or dried in the sun and pounded into flour.

The thick fleshy root consists almost entirely of starch, with less than one per cent protein, and less iron and B-complex vitamins than cereal grains contain. So people living in areas where cassava is the main staple food could suffer from protein and iron-deficiency diseases if they were poorly fed.

BANANAS

'Banana' is the African name for the fruit which came from South-East Asia to East Africa nearly a thousand years ago. Ancient legend says that the wise men of India rested under the shade of the plant and ate the fruit. The banana's name 'musa sapientium' means 'fruit of the wisemen'. In tropical Africa bananas are grown mainly as a cash crop for export. Each banana plant bears one stem carrying 100–200 bananas. Cooking bananas, called **plantains**, are a staple food in areas of East and West Africa.

Collecting oil palm fruits

Sorting cassava roots

GROUNDNUTS

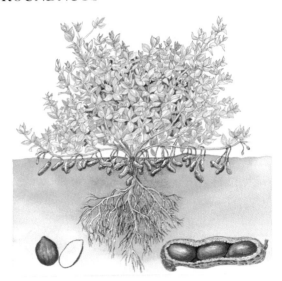

Groundnuts are also known as peanuts or earthnuts. They are grown in many tropical areas and are important as a food as well as for their oil.

The groundnut came from South America and in the sixteenth century Portuguese sailors took it across to Africa. Today groundnuts are cultivated in all areas of Africa south of the Sahara desert. Nigeria is the world's largest exporter of groundnuts.

The seeds are planted in rows and the plant has yellow flowers which turn into brown pods. These pods turn down into the ground and bury themselves below the surface. The plant is dug up at harvest time and the wrinkled pod which contains one or two nuts is removed.

In Nigeria, women shell the nuts by pounding them with a long wooden mortar. They keep some nuts for seed, some for cooking and making oil, and then sell the rest.

Groundnuts are eaten raw or roasted and are used in African cooking for stews and soups. They provide valuable protein, fat, and carbohydrate. Each nut contains 40–50 per cent oil, and this groundnut oil is made by squeezing the nuts between presses. The oil is a useful vegetable oil and is made into margarine, ice cream, and sweets.

Groundnuts are also crushed to make peanut butter. Try making your own.

◄ PEANUT BUTTER ►

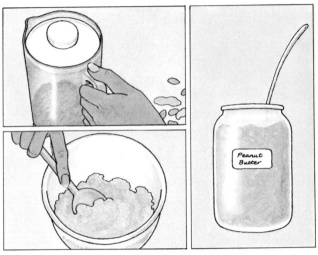

100 g roasted peanuts
vegetable oil if needed
salt

▼

1 Grind the nuts in a blender. A smooth butter is made by grinding the nuts finely, and a crunchy butter by grinding for less time.
2 At this stage the peanuts may press into a butter. If not, beat in a few drops of oil.
3 Add salt to taste and put the butter in a jar. The mixture should keep for several weeks but may need a stir before using.

Harvesting groundnuts

UGALI WITH BEEF
◄ AND VEGETABLE SOUP ►

This recipe comes from Kenya and uses maize and beef, both farmed in the area. Ugali is a cornmeal porridge eaten with soups and stews.

UGALI

200 g yellow cornmeal (maize flour)
500 ml water

1 Boil the water in a saucepan. Using a wooden spoon, stir in enough cornmeal to make a stiff pudding.
2 Beat well to avoid lumps, then cook for 2–3 minutes.

BEEF AND VEGETABLE SOUP

250 g minced beef
1 medium onion, peeled and chopped
1 large tomato, skinned and chopped
$\frac{1}{2}$ tsp chilli powder
$\frac{1}{2}$ tsp salt
200 g green cabbage, washed and finely chopped
1 tbs cornmeal flour
250 ml water

1 In a large saucepan, fry the mince and onion together, stirring with a wooden spoon, until the mince turns brown.
2 Add the tomato, cornmeal flour, chilli, and salt, then stir in the water.
3 Bring to the boil, lower the heat, then cover and cook for 20 minutes.
4 Add the chopped cabbage and cook for a further 5 minutes. Serve hot with ugali.

Serves 2–4.

◄ BOBOTIE ►

Bobotie is a traditional South African dish of curried mince with nuts and raisins, covered with a savoury custard.

1 large onion, finely chopped
1 tbs oil
1 thick slice of bread
250 ml milk
500 g minced beef or lamb
1 tbs curry powder
25 g flaked almonds (optional)
50 g raisins
1 tbs lemon juice
salt and pepper
2 eggs

1 Set the oven at 180°C/350°F/Gas 4.
2 Break the bread and soak it in half the milk.
3 Fry the onion in the oil until golden brown.
4 Using a fork, mix the meat with all the ingredients except the eggs and remaining milk. Spoon into the ovenproof dish.
5 Beat the eggs and remaining milk together and pour this over the meat. Bake for one hour until the mixture is set and lightly browned.

Serves 4.

◄ GROUNDNUT STEW ►

This chicken dish in a rich peanut sauce is eaten widely all over Africa. It may be served with rice, fufu, or boiled cassava.

1 kilo chicken portions
100 g peanut butter
2 large onions, peeled and finely chopped
1 medium can tomatoes, blended or sieved
1 tbs tomato purée
$\frac{1}{2}$ tsp chilli powder
$\frac{1}{2}$ tsp salt
2 bayleaves
1 tbs groundnut *or* vegetable oil

1 Remove the skin and fat from the chicken.
2 Place the chicken, oil, onions, salt and bay leaves in a large pan. Cover with a lid and cook gently for 5 minutes.
3 Pour in 500 ml water and bring to the boil. Stir in the peanut butter and chilli powder.
4 Cover and cook for a further 15 minutes.
5 Add the blended tomatoes and tomato purée. Stir well, then cover and simmer for 45 minutes.
6 Stir and taste the dish before serving hot.

Serves 4.

◄ FUFU ►

Fufu are dumplings made from pounded root vegetables such as cassava or yams, or from maize or potatoes. The dumplings accompany soups and stews, providing a starchy filler.

4 heaped tbs potato powder
500 ml water

1 Place the potato powder in a small pan. Using a wooden spoon, blend in half the water to make a smooth paste.
2 Cook the mixture over a low heat, stirring all the time. As it boils, beat in more water until the paste is thick and gluey. Cook for a further 5 minutes.
3 Scoop out tablespoons of the mixture and shape into 6–8 oval dumplings on a warmed dish. Serve.

◀ COUSCOUS ▶

Couscous, made from wheat, is the national dish of North Africa. Couscous is a fine semolina which has been mixed with water and made into small pellets like chopped rice. Couscous is cooked by steaming over meat and vegetable stews. Couscous can be bought from most big supermarkets.

200 g couscous
1 onion, peeled and chunked
2 carrots, peeled and cut into chunks
2 stalks of celery, scrubbed and chopped
400 g small cubes of lean stewing lamb
or 2 chicken portions
2 leeks
1 tbs tomato purée
50 g raisins
salt and pepper
½ tsp chilli powder
25 g butter

1 Soak the couscous in a bowl with 300 ml warm water for 10 minutes.
2 Meantime prepare the vegetables, except the leeks. Trim off fat from the lamb or chicken.

Place the vegetables and meat in a large pan, and just cover with water. Bring to the boil, then cover the pan with a lid and turn down the heat. Cook gently for 30 minutes.
3 Prepare the leeks – cut off the root, remove any damaged parts, then make a slit down the length of the leek. Clean under running water to wash out any soil, then cut into chunks.
4 Add the tomato purée, raisins, leeks, salt, pepper, and chilli to the stew. Stir well and continue cooking.
5 The couscous is cooked by steaming it above the level of the boiling stew. The couscous is placed in a metal sieve or colander lined with muslin, fitting into the top of the saucepan. Steam for 20–30 minutes with a lid on top. Make sure that the liquid from the stew does not touch the steamer as the couscous will become lumpy.
6 Stir the couscous with a fork before turning it out on to a large warmed plate. Dot with pieces of butter. Make a well in the centre and spoon in the meat and vegetables and some sauce.

Serves 4.

INDIA, PAKISTAN, AND BANGLADESH

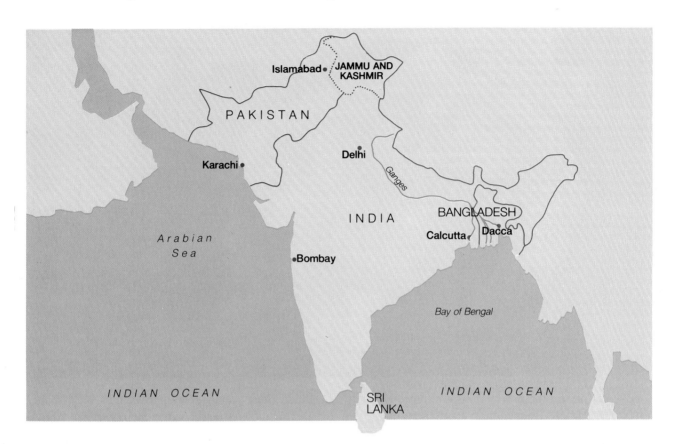

The vast subcontinent of India, Pakistan, and Bangladesh has great variations in climate, peoples, religions, and foods.

INDIA

India has a population of nearly 700 million and is an agricultural country with 70 per cent of the people working on the land. Important crops include wheat, rice, maize, and millet, as well as beans, lentils, spices, and tea. India is the world's largest producer of millet and groundnuts and the second largest grower of rice, sugar, and bananas.

More than half the people of India are vegetarians: some for religious reasons, but many because they cannot afford to buy meat or fish. Poorer people live on a diet of cereals, lentils, and vegetables, and a main meal may only consist of rice, dhal (lentils and beans), and some chilli peppers.

PAKISTAN

Pakistan became a separate Muslim state in 1947, and has a population of about 87 million. Much of the land is dry and hard to cultivate in the hot climate. The main crops are wheat and rice.

BANGLADESH

In 1971 East Pakistan became Bangladesh, a country with a population of about 92 million, mostly Muslim by religion. The country is almost entirely agricultural, the chief crops being rice, tea, and tobacco. The principal river of India, the Ganges, flows through Bangladesh to the sea and is liable to frequent flooding, ruining many of the crops grown nearby.

In India, Pakistan, and Bangladesh the chief religions which affect food customs are **Hinduism** and **Islam** (the religion of the Muslims). In Pakistan most people are Muslims and about 80 per cent of Indians are Hindus. Strict **Hindus** are vegetarians who believe that it is wrong to kill animals so they do not eat meat, fish, or eggs. Other Hindus do not eat beef since the cow is sacred to them, but they do eat lamb, poultry, fish, and sometimes pork. Milk and milk products are used.

Muslims may not eat pork or drink alcohol. Animals are specially slaughtered and sold as **halal** meat from special butchers.

Sikhs do not have any strict dietary rules, but many are vegetarians.

COOKING IN DIFFERENT AREAS

In northern India and Pakistan, food is often cooked in a clay oven called a **tandoor**, which is charcoal fired. Meat, usually lamb, goat, or chicken, is marinated in yoghurt and spices to make it more tender, then cooked quickly in the oven. The tandoor is used to cook a bread made with yeast, called **nan**.

In the north of India where wheat is the staple food, dishes are drier and may be scooped up using chapatis: round, flat breads made from wheat.

Rice is the staple food in southern India. More liquid curries are served in this area. The heavy rains help to produce a great variety of vegetables including aubergines, okra, and different sorts of pepper. Here many people are vegetarians.

Most Indian food is cooked on top of the stove and an oven is rarely used. Many freshly-ground spices are mixed and used to flavour Indian dishes. Indian cooks make up their own special blends of spices and don't use ready-made curry powder.

Cooking is done using **ghee** or vegetable oil. Ghee is made by heating butter, then leaving it to set. This is a way of preserving butter since ghee will not go rancid even in the hottest weather.

SERVING INDIAN MEALS

Eating habits in India are changing, but traditionally food was eaten with the right hand. Meals are served differently throughout India.

In central India small helpings from each dish are placed on a tray or **thali**. Dishes may include dhal, vegetable curries, relishes, and chapatis.

In the south, food such as curry and rice may be served on banana leaves. In northern India and Pakistan, all the dishes are placed on the table at once, and everyone helps themselves.

67

SOME INDIAN VEGETABLES

OKRA (LADY'S FINGERS OR GUMBO)

Okra grows throughout the Indian sub-continent and may be served on its own as a vegetable or as part of a dish. Okra are five-sided green pods which are finger size – hence the name 'lady's fingers'! They should be picked young, and the stalk end needs removing, but the pod should not be cut as the vegetable will become sticky. Cook gently by boiling or frying.

AUBERGINE OR EGG PLANT

Aubergines are used in many Indian dishes to add flavour and colour. The aubergine originated in tropical Asia and grows in several shapes – it may be long, oval, or round, and it varies in colour from white to green to purple. Aubergines may be sliced and boiled, fried, or added to curries and other dishes.

DID YOU KNOW?

Indians eat silver and gold! On festival days very finely-beaten gold and silver leaf are used to decorate puddings and sweets.

Curry is not a word used by Indians. Each dish has a name according to the ingredients used. The term 'curry' probably came from **kari**, the Indian word for sauce.

INDIAN TEA

Picking tea in Darjeeling

India is the largest tea exporter in the world. Tea grows on an evergreen tropical bush and the young shoots and buds are picked for the tea. Tea needs a warm, wet climate and a well-drained soil. Teas grown at higher altitudes are usually of better quality than teas from the plains.

In India there are three important tea areas: **Darjeeling** in the foothills of the Himalayas produces a rare, delicate tea which makes up only three per cent of India's total tea production.

Assam in northern India has rolling plains and is one of the largest tea-growing areas in the world. Assam tea is strong and used for blending with other teas.

Nilgiri in southern India grows a tea of delicate flavour.

SPICES

Indian food uses a wide variety of spices from around the world to add colour and flavour to dishes. In the past spices were valuable because they were used to preserve food such as meats and to make pickles and chutneys.

CORIANDER

Coriander is the most widely-used herb/spice in the world and has been cultivated for thousands of years. The seed (the spice) is crushed and used in Indian curries and the fresh leaves (the herb) flavour food from the Middle East and Greece.

CUMIN

Cumin is grown for its seeds which are ground and used in curry powder. The whole seed is used in breads and vegetable dishes.

CHILLI POWDER

Chilli powder is made from dried red chilli peppers, ground to a powder. It can vary from mild to very hot and is used in curries and hot Mexican and South American dishes. Fresh green chillies are used in many Indian recipes.

GINGER

Ginger is an underground stem or rhizome native to tropical Asia. It is known as root ginger. It is available fresh or dried and ground. Fresh ginger is used in Indian and Oriental cooking and needs peeling, chopping, or grating before use.

TURMERIC

Turmeric is the dried underground stem or rhizome of a plant. It may be used whole or ground into an orange-yellow powder to give flavour and colour to curries and chutneys. It is sometimes used instead of saffron.

CARDAMOM

Cardamom is the world's most expensive spice after saffron. The dried fruit consists of three capsules containing seeds. Cardamom is used to flavour rice dishes and even coffee. It tastes slightly lemony and may be crushed before using in cooking.

PULSES

Pulses are the edible seeds of certain plants including peas, beans, and lentils. All types of pulses are good sources of protein and carbohydrate. They also contain B-complex vitamins, iron, and fibre. Some beans contain toxic chemicals so it is wise to boil all beans for ten minutes before using them in a recipe.

RED KIDNEY BEANS ①

These beans range in colour from pink to maroon and are popular in Mexican cooking. The raw bean is poisonous and must be boiled for ten minutes to destroy the toxin.

WHITE BEANS ②

These are a variety of haricot beans. They come in different sizes but all have the same kidney shape. American white beans, called **navy beans**, were used to supply the navy. White beans are often canned in tomato sauce.

BUTTER BEANS ③

Butter beans are large, flat, white beans, traditionally used in British cooking.

BLACK-EYED BEANS ④

Also called **cow peas**, these beans are small and white with a black or yellow 'eye'. They are used in many countries and popular in the USA.

SOYA BEANS ⑤

These are small and oval in shape and may be yellow, green, red, or black. They are important in Chinese cooking where they are made into soy sauce and beancurd.

MUNG BEANS ⑥

Mung beans are tiny green beans which may be used whole, split, or skinless. The Chinese sprout mung beans for beansprouts.

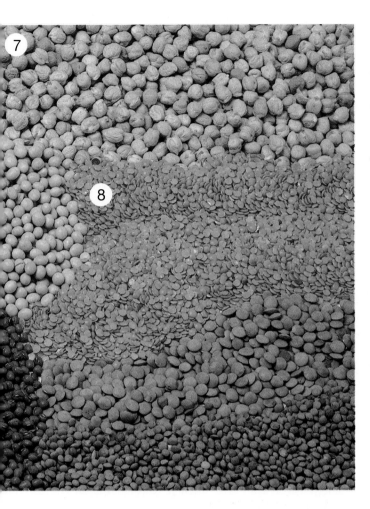

Dhal, made from lentils, is an important part of the basic diet of most Indians. Lentils provide a cheap source of protein, especially for vegetarians. There are many varieties of lentils grown in India. They come in different sizes and shapes and so cooking times vary. Dhal is eaten with bread and rice, sometimes spiced with hot chillies.

175 g yellow split lentils
700 ml water
1 tsp turmeric
1 green chilli (optional)
1 clove of garlic, peeled and crushed
1 small onion, finely chopped
1 tsp cumin seeds
50 g ghee, butter, *or* 2 tbs vegetable oil

▼

1 Tip the lentils on to a plate and pick out any stones or strange items! Wash the lentils in a sieve.
2 Place the lentils in a pan with the water and turmeric. Bring to the boil, then lower the heat, partly cover, and simmer for 45 minutes. Stir occasionally and remove any scum which forms.
3 Meanwhile prepare the chilli. Either use it whole and remove after cooking, *or* chop finely. Use the seeds if a very hot dish is preferred. Add the chilli to the dhal.
   Remember: Never rub your face or eyes when preparing chillies as the juices sting. Wash your hands afterwards.
4 Heat the ghee, butter, *or* oil in a pan and fry the cumin seeds, onion, and garlic until the onion is golden. Stir this into the lentils and season with salt. Serve hot with rice or to accompany other dishes.

Note: lentils and pulses are not cooked in salt as salt lengthens cooking time and tends to stop the beans softening.

CHICK-PEAS ⑦

Chick-peas are large peas shaped like hazel-nuts which are usually beige or golden in colour. They have a nutty flavour and crunchy texture. Chick-peas are eaten whole, ground into flour, or made into dips such as **hummus**. They are used in Indian, Middle Eastern, and Oriental cooking.

LENTILS ⑧

There are many varieties of lentil, each named after their colour – yellow, orange, green, brown, and black. They are flattish and round in shape and vary in size. Lentils may be used whole or split and are important in Indian cooking as a main or side dish with curry. They usually do not require soaking before cooking.

INDIAN BREADS

Bread and rice are the most important foods in India. Most breads are cooked on top of the stove and freshly made without using yeast. There are several types of bread:

Chapatis, the most popular type of bread, are round and flat.
Puris are small round breads, deep fried.
Parathas are heavier, layered breads, sometimes stuffed with vegetables.
Phulkas are deep fried, puffed-up breads.
Nan, usually made with yeast, is oven-baked.

Cooking chapatis

nan

chapatis

puris

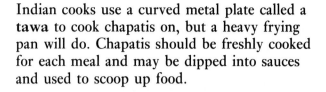

Indian cooks use a curved metal plate called a **tawa** to cook chapatis on, but a heavy frying pan will do. Chapatis should be freshly cooked for each meal and may be dipped into sauces and used to scoop up food.

200 g wholewheat flour
1 tsp salt
125 ml water

1 Sieve the flour and salt into a large bowl. Using your hands, gradually work in the water to form a stiff dough. Add more flour or water if the mixture is difficult to handle.
2 Place the dough in a ball on the work surface and knead with your hands for 5 minutes to make the dough smooth and elastic.
3 Cover the dough with plastic film or a damp tea-towel and leave it to rest for 30 minutes.
4 Roll the dough into a sausage shape and divide into 12 equal pieces. Sprinkle some flour on the work surface and shape each piece into a ball. Flatten and roll into a circle 12 – 15 cm in diameter.
5 Heat the frying pan until it is very hot. If necessary use a little oil to prevent the chapati sticking. Cook the chapati for one minute until small bubbles appear on the top.
6 Turn over and cook the other side for another minute.
7 Traditionally, the chapati is held over an open flame to puff it up, but this can be dangerous. Instead, heat the chapati quickly under a hot grill.
8 Serve immediately and keep hot by wrapping in a warm tea-towel.

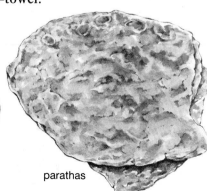

parathas

72

◀ VEGETABLE PULAO ▶

Pulaos are dry rice dishes cooked with other ingredients. They can be served as the main dish or as part of a meal.

50 g ghee *or* butter *or* 2 tbs oil
1 onion, finely chopped
1 clove of garlic, crushed
200 g long grain rice
1 potato, peeled and chunked
1 carrot, peeled and diced
50 g fresh green beans (optional)
or 50 g frozen peas
1 tsp salt
$\frac{1}{2}$ tsp each of turmeric, cumin, and coriander
$\frac{1}{2}$ tsp chilli powder
$\frac{1}{2}$ litre of water

1 Heat the ghee, butter, or oil in a pan and fry the onion until soft. Add the spices and garlic and fry for 2–3 minutes, then stir in the rice and vegetables. Cook for 5 minutes.
2 Pour over the water and bring to the boil. Stir and cover tightly with foil and a lid. Cook very slowly for 40 minutes. Serve hot.

Serves 4.

◀ CRUNCHY RELISH ▶

Simple relishes called **sambals** are served with main meals to add colour and texture.

2 medium sliced tomatoes
1 onion, peeled and sliced in rings
1 tbs chopped coriander leaves *or* parsley
juice of $\frac{1}{2}$ lemon *or* 2 tbs lemon juice
$\frac{1}{2}$ tsp salt

▼

Mix all the ingredients together and spoon into a serving dish.

◀ CHICKEN PALAK ▶

This spicy chicken dish is cooked in a sauce with tomatoes and spinach.

50 g ghee *or* butter *or* 4 tbs oil
225 g fresh *or* frozen spinach
4 chicken pieces, skinned and defatted
2 cm piece of fresh ginger, peeled and grated
and 1 green chilli, finely chopped
or $\frac{1}{4}$ tsp each of ground ginger and chilli powder
1 large onion, peeled and finely chopped
1 clove of garlic, peeled and crushed
1 tsp salt
2 tsp each of cumin and coriander
1 medium can (about 400 g) of chopped tomatoes

▼

1 Wash the spinach well and chop finely.
2 In a large pan fry the chicken pieces in the fat until golden brown on each side.
3 Remove the chicken and fry the onion in the same pan until it browns. Add the spices – garlic, ginger, chilli, cumin, coriander – and cook for a further 2–3 minutes.
4 Stir in the fresh or frozen spinach, salt, and can of tomatoes. Add the chicken pieces.
5 Cover and cook on a low heat for 45 minutes, stirring occasionally. Add some water if the sauce begins to dry up.
6 Serve hot with rice, chapatis, and dhal.
Serves 4.

◀ BANANA RAITA ▶

Refreshing raitas made from yoghurt are served with spicy dishes and help 'cool' the meal. Raitas can be made from different vegetables such as potatoes, cucumber, and chick-peas.

1 banana, peeled and thinly sliced
150 g natural yoghurt

Mix all the ingredients together and serve chilled.

◀ ZARDA ▶

In India, a meal may be followed by fruit and sometimes a pudding such as zarda.

150 g short grain rice
50 g ghee *or* butter
2 cardamoms, crushed
2 cloves
1 small stick of cinnamon
or ½ tsp ground cinnamon
300 ml milk
50 g sugar
50 g raisins

1 Boil the rice in a large pan with plenty of water for 10 minutes. Drain the rice.
2 Melt the butter or ghee and fry the rice, cloves, cinnamon, and crushed cardamom. Add the milk and sugar and cook for 5 minutes until the rice is soft.
3 Stir in the raisins and either cook the rice gently for 20 minutes on top of the stove or turn into a dish and cook in a low oven. Serve the rice hot or cold.

Serves 2–4.

◀ LASSI ▶

Lassi is a delicious yoghurt drink sold in markets and bazaars. It can be served by itself or with an Indian meal. Use salt and pepper instead of sugar if you prefer a savoury drink.

2 small cartons (about 300 g) natural yoghurt
600 ml ice cold water
juice of ½ lemon
2 tsp sugar

1 Either use a liquidizer or whisk all the ingredients until frothy.
2 Pour into glasses and serve.
Serves 4.

DID YOU KNOW?

Sometimes at the end of an Indian meal, a small package called **paan** is chewed to help the digestion and freshen the mouth. Paan is made from strange ingredients. A betel leaf is folded round different spices such as cardamom, betel nut, and aniseed. It is then shaped into a triangle and sealed. Marco Polo, the explorer, said the Indians had 'capital teeth owing to this herb they chew'.

CHINA

China is the third largest country in the world next to the USSR and Canada, and has the world's greatest population to support – over a billion people.

Most people work on the land, growing wheat and maize in the north, and rice and soya beans in the south. Northern people make wheat into

Selling eels in China

noodles, dumplings, and steamed rolls. Rice is the main carbohydrate food in the south and people may eat as much as 750 g a day.

Farmers keep pigs, ducks, and chickens, but few cattle since there is little grazing land. In coastal areas the Chinese have been eating fish for six thousand years. They learned to rear fish in special fish farms nearly two centuries ago.

Selling chickens' feet in Hong Kong

CHINESE FOOD CUSTOMS

The Chinese eat almost anything. Markets sell strange foods such as snakes, locusts, and chicken's and duck's feet. There is a Chinese saying that they will 'eat anything with wings except an aeroplane, and anything with four legs except a table'!

Cooking follows simple rules. Cook what is fresh, use as little fuel as possible, and stir so that the food cooks quickly and evenly. Chinese food is often flavoured with root ginger, garlic, spring onions, and of course, soy sauce.

Many Chinese live on a largely vegetarian diet. Religious groups such as Buddhists and Taoists encourage their followers to become vegetarians.

The Chinese believe that everything you eat has an important effect on the body, something scientists in the West have only considered in the last hundred years.

76

MEAL TIMES

For family meals the Chinese sit round a table and four or five dishes are served at once. Each person has their own rice bowl and uses chopsticks to help themselves to the other foods. Soup may be served at any point during the meal, eaten from bowls with porcelain spoons. The meal may end with fruit, and tea is usually drunk with the meal.

CHOPSTICKS

The Chinese were using chopsticks when other people were still eating with their fingers. Have a go yourself:

1 Hold the thick end of the chopstick, resting the top end between the thumb and first finger, and the middle on the third finger. This chopstick should not move.

2 The second chopstick, which does move, is held by the first finger and the thumb, like a pencil. The tips of the chopsticks should meet.

3 Wiggle the top chopstick with the finger and thumb, and the tips of the chopsticks should pinch together. Now try picking things up!

Since you can only pick up small pieces of food with chopsticks, each flavour can be enjoyed. With knives and forks the flavours and foods are all mixed up together.

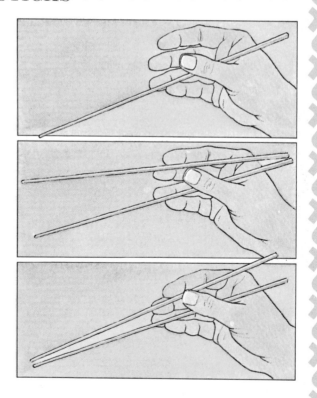

Remember: never cross your chopsticks when you lay them down. You will bring bad luck to your host!

CHINESE-STYLE VEGETABLE PREPARATION

The Chinese prepare their vegetables carefully to make food look attractive.

Diagonal cutting – celery, carrots, courgettes, and spring onions can be cut at a slant into thin slices.

Spring onion brushes – trim off the root and top, leaving 7 cm of stem. Make four crossing cuts 2 cm deep at each end. Place in cold water to open out, then use for decoration.

Strip cutting – cut the vegetables into long diagonal slices, then cut each slice into 2–3 strips.

Carrot flowers – peel a thick carrot and cut V-shaped grooves lengthways evenly round the carrot. Cut into slices.

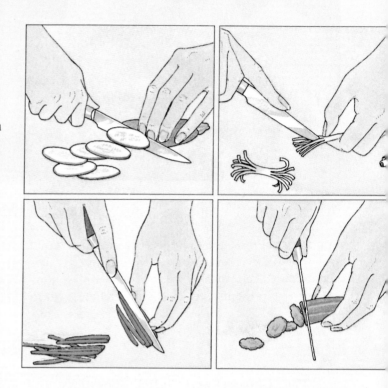

THE WOK

Wood and other fuels have long been scarce in China, and baking ovens are rarely found. Five thousand years ago the Chinese designed the **wok** – an iron pan with a curved bottom which cooks food very quickly, saving precious fuel. The roundness of the wok allows food to be scooped and stirred more easily than it can be in a saucepan. The wok is used for steaming and deep-fat frying as well as stir-frying.

Woks blacken with use and need to be greased before they are put away. An old Chinese proverb says 'the blacker the wok, the better the cook'.

Stir-frying cooks food quickly, keeping vegetables crunchy and conserving nutrients, especially vitamin C. More time is spent preparing than cooking and everything should be cut into pieces of roughly the same size. The Chinese chop with a cleaver on a slice of tree trunk, but sharp knives and a chopping board will do instead.

Deep-fat frying in a wok

CHINESE FRUIT AND VEGETABLES

CHINESE LEAVES

This tall, pale green vegetable looks like a Cos lettuce with white stems. The leaves are chopped for Chinese salads and stir-fry dishes.

THE LOTUS PLANT

This fresh-water vegetable grows on Chinese lakes and looks like a water lily. The root is boiled or steamed, then peeled and sliced. Each slice has a pattern of holes like a doily, and tastes like potato. The **seeds** are eaten and the **leaves** are used to wrap round food for steaming.

WATER-CHESTNUTS

These bulb-like vegetables grow on shallow lakes and marshes. They are peeled and sliced to give crunchiness to salads and stir-fry dishes. They can be bought in cans.

BAMBOO SHOOTS

The crunchy texture of bamboo shoots is popular in stir-fry dishes. The creamy inner part of the young bamboo shoot is boiled and sliced before cooking. They may be canned.

LYCHEES

This juicy white fruit may be eaten at the end of a meal. Lychees are the size of small plums, with a brittle red skin which is peeled away. The small brown seed in the middle is covered by the delicate white flesh. They may be canned.

KIWI FRUIT

The kiwi fruit or Chinese gooseberry came from China but is now grown in many countries. The hairy skin may be removed before eating. The green flesh looks attractive sliced up in fruit salads.

Planting out rice seedlings in China

Rice is one of man's oldest foods – the Chinese have been growing rice for over 4000 years. From China, travellers took rice to India and South-East Asia, and now it is cultivated in many parts of the world. The Chinese are the world's largest rice producers, growing 155 million tons – 30 per cent of the world output.

HOW RICE IS GROWN AND HARVESTED

Rice grows well in hot countries with a high rainfall and suitable soil. In Asia, rice is a valuable cereal since farmers can raise two crops a year.

Apart from upland rice which grows like other cereals, most rice is grown in flooded fields called **paddies**. Entire families wade out to plant rice seedlings which grow under water for several weeks. When the crop has grown about a metre high and ripened, the water is drained from the paddy fields, leaving them ready for harvesting.

In many countries, including China, rice is still harvested by hand using knives. After drying and threshing to sort out the grains, the rice is cleaned. Then the outside husk is removed, leaving brown rice. White polished rice can be produced by milling the brown rice to remove the bran, then polishing the grain.

In more advanced countries such as the USA, aeroplanes are used to sow the seeds, and machinery helps water the land and harvest the crop.

THE NUTRITIONAL VALUE OF RICE

Rice is the staple food for over half the world's population and many people throughout China and Indonesia eat little else.

Brown rice is nutritious, providing carbohydrate for energy, a little protein for body growth, minerals such as calcium, and vitamins, especially the B-complex vitamins thiamin and niacin.

Polished white rice has had the 'silver skin' of the rice grain removed. The skin contains most of the thiamin, and so white rice is deficient in this vitamin. Polished white rice is popular since it is quicker to cook and keeps longer.

Rice-growing areas

TYPES OF RICE

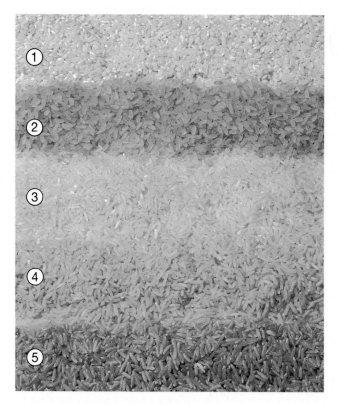

With so many varieties of rice, different countries have their own favourites.

① **Short grain rice** is eaten by Western countries for milky puddings. **Short grain sticky rice** is popular in Japan and East Asia. The grains cling together in a sticky mass when cooked.

② **Medium grain rice** is used for Italian risotto. The grains are less sticky than pudding rice.

③ **Long grain rice** has long, slim grains which remain firm and fluffy when cooked. This rice is served with savoury dishes, It is used in Chinese and Indian cooking. **Patna** and **Basmati** rice are the most popular long grain rice.

④ **Basmati rice** is grown in the foothills of the Himalayas and is considered to be the finest rice. The word 'basmati' means 'the fragrant one' and this rice has a delicious flavour and smell when cooked.

⑤ **Brown rice** has only the outer husk removed and has a nutty flavour and chewy texture. The rice may be long or short grain, and takes longer to cook – usually about 20–25 minutes.

HOW TO COOK RICE

Rice needs no preparation and can be boiled and cooked in 11–20 minutes. It is one of the world's oldest convenience foods! The Chinese have several ways of cooking rice. This is one of them.

2 teacups full of long grain rice
4 teacups full of water (same size cups)

1 Wash the rice in a strainer under running water.
2 Boil the water in a large pan, then stir in the rice with a fork. Let the water come back to the boil, then turn down the heat to the lowest setting and cover the pan with a lid.
3 Let the rice cook for 20 minutes without lifting the lid. Turn off the heat and let the rice stand for a few minutes. Remove the lid, fluff up the rice with a fork, and it is ready to serve.

DID YOU KNOW?

Throwing paper confetti at weddings is a modern version of the ancient Chinese custom of throwing rice at newly-weds. The Chinese believed that the rice would help the couple have many children.

BEAN SPROUTS

The Chinese have been sprouting beans for thousands of years. Chinese bean sprouts are grown from mung beans but other beans, such as aduki beans and chick-peas can be sprouted too.

Bean sprouts must be the freshest vegetables we eat, since they are still growing when they are served. They are nutritious too, providing vitamins C and B-complex, a little protein, and fibre.

Try growing your own bean sprouts.
You will need:
50 g mung beans, soaked overnight
either
a large jam jar, some cloth, and an elastic band
or
a colander, lined and covered with an old tea-towel

1 Wash the beans, removing any that are damaged. Place in the jar or colander and find a place away from draughts and sunlight.
2 Two or three times a day pour warm water over the beans, then drain it off. Leave the jar on its side, slightly tilted to remove excess water.
3 Repeat every day for 3–5 days until the sprouts are 3–5 cm high. If you are lucky you can grow 200 g bean sprouts from 50 g beans.

Remember: don't forget to water the beans and remove any that go mouldy. Home-grown mung beans are greener than shop-bought beans which are grown in the dark.

CHINESE TEA

Chinese legend says that tea was discovered by the Emperor Shen-Hung. As he sat by a wild tea plant, some leaves fell into his pot of boiling water. He had a taste and found it delicious – and so tea-drinking began.

In China, tea is known as 'cha' and it is drunk everywhere at any time of day. China tea is drunk without milk, sugar, or lemon. There are two main types of tea:
Green tea is picked and quickly dried. It has a greenish colour and a mild flavour.
Black tea is darker and stronger in flavour because the leaves have been fermented.

LIVER
◄ AND WATERCRESS SOUP ►

This soup is cheap, yet delicious. It may be served at any time during a Chinese meal.

1 litre water
2 chicken stock cubes
75 g pig's or lamb's liver
1 bunch watercress

▼

1 Put the water and stock cubes in a large saucepan and bring to the boil.
2 Cut the liver into thin slivers and drop into the boiling water. Cook for 2 minutes, stirring with a wooden spoon.
3 Wash the watercress under running water, chop it roughly, and stir it into the soup. Bring the soup back to the boil, then it is ready to serve.

Serves 4.

CHINESE VEGETABLES
◄ AND NOODLES ►

400 g Chinese noodles or spaghetti
1 stick celery
1 carrot
5–6 tbs bean sprouts
50 g bamboo shoots (optional)
50 g mushrooms
50 g Chinese leaves, shredded
2 tbs vegetable oil
2 tbs soy sauce

Garnish
1 tbs oil
4 spring onions, sliced

▼

1 Boil the noodles for 7–8 minutes in a large pan of water. (Spaghetti takes about 15 minutes.) Drain and rinse with water.
2 Peel the carrot and wash the other vegetables. Cut the celery, carrot, mushrooms, and bamboo shoots into thin slivers.
3 Heat the oil in the wok or pan and stir-fry all the vegetables except the bean sprouts. Cook over a high heat for 2 minutes, then add the bean sprouts and cook a further 1 minute. Add the noodles and soy sauce, lower the heat, and turn the noodles gently to warm through. After 3–4 minutes pile the noodles on to a dish.
4 Wipe out the wok with kitchen towel. Add the extra oil, then stir-fry the spring onions for one minute. Spoon them over the noodles.

Serves 4.

84

◄ FRIED RICE ►

Fried rice originated as a way of using up left-over rice and has become a dish in itself. A variety of different ingredients may be added. Fried rice can be served with other savoury foods or eaten as a meal on its own.

2 tbs vegetable oil
4 rashers of bacon with rind removed
1 onion, peeled and finely chopped
2 spring onions, sliced diagonally (see page 78)
400 g cooked rice
100 g frozen peas
1 tbs soy sauce
2 eggs
salt and pepper

▼

1 Cut the bacon into matchstick strips. Beat together the eggs, salt, and pepper, using a fork.
2 Heat the oil in a wok or large saucepan. Stir-fry the onion and bacon for 2 minutes. Add the spring onion and peas.
3 Stir in the rice, mix in the soy sauce, and cook for a further 5 minutes, stirring all the time.
4 Pour the beaten egg into the rice in a thin stream, stirring all the time. Cook for 1–2 minutes until the egg is cooked.
5 Serve the rice hot or cold.

Serves 4.

RED COOKED ◄ CHICKEN ►

Red cooked chicken is coloured dark brown by soy sauce.

2 large chicken breast portions (about 400 g)
2 cm root ginger
2 tbs soy sauce
1 tsp sugar

▼

1 Skin the chicken and cut the flesh into chunks. Put the chicken and bones in a large pan and just cover with boiling water.
2 Add the root ginger, soy sauce, and sugar.
3 Cover with a tight-fitting lid and simmer for an hour until tender. Remove the ginger.
4 Remove the bones, cutting off any flesh.
5 Serve with boiled rice and stir-fried vegetables.

Stir-fried vegetables: choose 450 g of mixed vegetables – spring onions, bean sprouts, celery, and courgettes, for example.
Heat 2 tbs oil in a wok or pan, then stir and toss the vegetables with a wooden spoon for 3–4 minutes. Add 1 tbs soy sauce, toss once more, then serve.

Serves 4.

◀ SWEET AND SOUR PORK ▶

Originally from southern China, this is one of the most famous Chinese dishes.

300 g lean pork
2 courgettes, washed and cut into chunks
1 carrot, peeled, cut into chunks,
then left in boiling
water for 4 minutes
1 red or green pepper,
deseeded and cut into chunks
1 orange, peeled and cut into segments

Batter
1 egg
2 level tbs cornflour
vegetable oil for deep frying

Sauce
2 tbs cider vinegar
1 tbs soy sauce
1 tbs tomato paste
1 tbs brown sugar
200 ml water
1 level tsp cornflour

Garnish
2 spring onions, sliced

1 Cut the pork into bite-size pieces.
2 Mix the egg and cornflour for the batter, using a fork. Dip each piece of pork into this mixture.
3 Heat 4 cm oil in a wok or large saucepan. Put one piece of meat into the oil: if it sizzles, the oil is ready. Fry a few pieces of meat at a time, until golden brown. Drain the meat and set aside. When cool carefully strain out the oil.
Remember: never leave food when it is frying, and keep a lid handy to put out a fire.
4 Cut all the vegetables to the same size as the pork pieces. The Chinese like harmony and 'sameness' with ingredients in a dish and this leads to even cooking.
5 Clean out the wok or pan and heat up 2 tbs oil, then stir-fry the vegetables. Cook the carrots and courgettes first, then the pepper and orange. Cook for 2 minutes altogether, then remove.
6 Pour all the sauce ingredients into the wok and stir rapidly to blend together. Then add the pork and vegetables, cover, and cook for a further 4–5 minutes.
7 Serve decorated with chopped spring onions and bowls of boiled rice.

Serves 4.

JAPAN ....

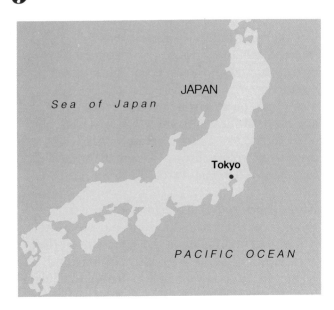

Even young Japanese people often eat in traditional style

Japan is a country made up of many islands stretching along the eastern coasts of China and Korea. The countryside is mountainous, with nearly 85 per cent of the land unsuitable for cultivation. With a population of nearly 117 million, Japan is a crowded country and it is difficult to grow enough food for everyone. Japan has become a leading industrial nation, exporting goods to help import food.

Since China and Japan are so close, they share many customs, such as sitting on the floor for meals and using chopsticks; and many foods, such as rice, noodles, and soya bean dishes. The appearance of Japanese food is however different from that of Chinese food, since the Japanese delight in presenting food like a work of art. Food is cut into larger pieces and the Japánese do not use a wok for cooking.

The Japanese have several bowls of rice with each meal. The average Japanese eat nearly one and a half kilograms of rice a week! They also eat many types of noodles made from buckwheat, potatoes, and wheat, and noodles are sold on the streets as snacks.

For a main family meal in Japan, all the dishes are placed on the table at once and everyone helps themselves. The meal may include a fish dish, plenty of rice, soup, and fruit, but no pudding. The family may drink tea or beer, or Japanese rice wine, **sake**.

TIMES ARE CHANGING

The Japanese enjoy trying out new ideas from other countries. Western customs are fashionable and more meals are now taken sitting on chairs at a table, using a knife and fork. Few people ate beef until recently but children are now trying hamburgers, chips, and pizzas.

With these richer foods the Japanese are growing taller and heavier, yet they still prefer their healthier low-fat diet of dishes of rice, fish, and soya beans.

Changes in height and weight of the average 20-year-old Japanese:

	Height		Weight	
	Men	Women	Men	Women
1960	161 cm	151 cm	55 kg	50 kg
1980	169 cm	156 cm	61 kg	51 kg

For centuries fish has been an important food for the Japanese. Since Buddhism was introduced during the seventh and eighth centuries, many Japanese have observed the rules of not eating flesh from 'four-footed animals'. Although many people do now eat meat, the Japanese enjoy a wonderful variety of fish.

The waters around Japan form one of the richest fishing grounds in the Pacific. The catch includes herring, sardine, tuna, and bonito – a type of mackerel.

However, to meet the increasing demand for food, one out of every ten fish eaten in Japan has been hatched and reared in salt or fresh water fish farms. Fish is becoming an expensive food to buy.

Sashimi, with flowers carved from vegetables

Fish may be cooked, salted, or dried, but in Japan the most popular way to serve fish is raw. There are two types of raw fish dishes and only very fresh fish can be used:
Sushi are little packages of raw fish and vinegared rice, sometimes with a little seaweed.
Sashimi are slices of raw fish served with shredded radish and seaweed. Using chopsticks the fish is dipped in soy sauce and **wasabi** – a hot horseradish sauce.

The Japanese visit restaurants to eat sushi and sashimi, since the preparation of these delicacies is a skilled job, requiring several years training.

The Japanese use many types of **seaweed** for cooking. Seaweed is rich in iodine which probably protects the Japanese from the disease **goitre**, a swelling of the thyroid gland in the neck, which is caused by lack of iodine.

Nori, dulse, caragheen, and arame

DID YOU KNOW?

The ugly-looking globe fish, **fugu**, secretes poison from its glands. The chef must not pierce a gland when preparing slices of the raw fish, since the flesh will be poisoned. Nearly 200 people a year die from eating poisoned globe fish.

SOYA BEANS

In Japan as well as China, cooks have invented many uses for the soya bean beyond that of simple boiling.

Soy sauce is a basic Japanese seasoning.
Miso, a soya bean paste, was originally made in China, but it is very popular in Japan. It looks like peanut butter, and may be yellow to deep reddish-brown in colour. Miso is used like stock cubes to flavour soups, stews, and dips.
Tofu is a mild-flavoured bean curd, a vegetable cheese which looks like white oblong blancmange. In Japan it is eaten on its own, with salads and stews, or sliced and fried. Tofu is an important source of protein and contains little fat. In Japan tofu is sold in shops or from barrows. Try making your own. First you need to make or buy soya milk.

◀ SOYA MILK ▶

275 g soya beans
1½ litres water

1 Soak the beans for 24 hours in cold water.
2 Drain and place the beans in a saucepan, adding 1½ litres of water. Bring to the boil and simmer for 15 minutes. Cool, pour into the blender, and blend until completely smooth. Pour the mixture into a fine cloth or clean pair of tights and squeeze out the soya milk.

◀ TOFU ▶

750 ml soya milk (bought or made)
1 level tbs Epsom salts + 1 tbs warm water
or 3 tbs cider vinegar

1 Boil the soya milk for 3 minutes, then remove from the heat.
2 Dissolve the Epsom salts in the water (*or* use vinegar) and stir quickly into the milk. Leave for 5–10 minutes while the milk thickens into curds, then place the curds in a fine cloth and strain out the liquid. Wrap the cloth around the curd, place on a dish, then cover with a saucer and a weight. Leave to drain for 2–3 hours.
3 Tofu can be stored for up to a week if it is kept in water in the fridge. Change the water daily.

◄ SUKIYAKI ►

The Japanese gather together round a table to cook sukiyaki using a portable gas or electric ring. A choice of thinly-sliced raw ingredients is laid out, and guests choose some of these to cook in a mixture of water, soy sauce, and sugar (the Japanese add sake, a rice wine). When the dish is ready, each person uses chop-sticks to take out a titbit, which they then dip in beaten egg before eating. Sukiyaki is usually served with plain boiled rice.

For sukiyaki you will need:

A sauce made of:

300 ml water
7 tbs soy sauce
2 tbs sugar

A plate of thinly-sliced raw foods such as:

whole mushrooms	bean sprouts
sliced Chinese cabbage	watercress
spring onions	quick-cook noodles
soya bean curd	slices of onion
sliced carrot	slivers of frying beef

1 egg for dipping

1 Heat up all the sauce ingredients together.
2 Heat up some oil in a pan and then stir in the beef using chopsticks. Cook for a few minutes.
3 Add a selection of vegetables.
4 Add 150 ml sauce to the pan.
5 Beat one egg in a little bowl for yourself.
6 Add the noodles, stir with chopsticks, cover, and cook for one minute.
7 The sukiyaki is ready. Dip pieces of food into your bowl of egg and eat.
8 As the pan empties, add more meat and vegetables to cook in the same way.

Eating sukiyaki in a restaurant

DID YOU KNOW?

For nearly four hundred years the Japanese have practised the tea ceremony. Both guest and host observe special rules. Powdered green tea is whisked into boiling water using a bamboo whisk. Cakes are eaten before the tea is served and to conclude, the teacup is turned upside down.

INDONESIA

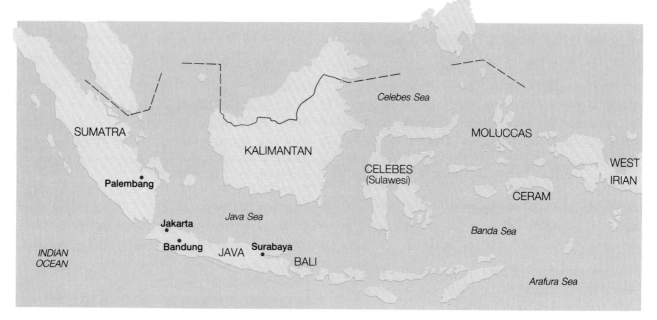

Thirteen thousand islands stretching either side of the equator make up the Republic of Indonesia. The population of 150 million lives mainly on the mountainous islands of Java, Bali, Sumatra, and Celebes. The climate is warm and wet and the land fertile. Eighty per cent of the people work on the land, many growing only enough to feed their families.

Rice is the most important food, providing two good crops a year. Farmers also grow cassava, soya beans, maize, groundnuts, and sugar. Coconuts and spices grow wild. Pastureland is scarce, so meat is expensive, although chickens are popular. Fish is one of Indonesia's main sources of protein, and fresh-water fish are sometimes bred in flooded paddy fields growing rice.

HISTORY

For centuries people have sailed the South Seas and China Seas and traded with the islands. The Malays arrived first, followed by the Chinese, the Indians, then the Arabs who converted many of the inhabitants to the Muslim faith – 90 per cent of Indonesians are now Muslims. By the sixteenth century, Europeans had come to trade, and for the next three hundred years the islands became the Dutch East Indies, controlled from Holland. Indonesia became independent in 1945.

The different visitors brought with them their own ways of cooking and eating. Hot spicy foods were introduced by the Indians, and food is cooked over a charcoal stove using a **wok** (see page 78) – a Chinese cooking pan. As in China, ovens are almost unknown and food is steamed, stir-fried, or boiled. Traditionally food was eaten with the right hand like the Arabs do, but nowadays a spoon and fork are used.

Everyday meals consist of rice with one or two vegetable dishes and a meat or fish dish, all served at once. A celebration meal serves many dishes. During Dutch rule these feasts were called the 'rice table', which today is often served in Indonesian restaurants around the world.

A market in Java

A spice market in Jakarta

The spices nutmeg, cloves, and pepper grow wild on the Indonesian islands called the Moluccas, better known as the Spice Islands. In the days before refrigeration, spices were very valuable. They were used to preserve food. Their strong flavour helped to hide the 'off' taste of old food. People used them for medicines and thought they protected them from diseases such as the plague.

The Moluccas were once the only islands in the world where cloves and nutmegs grew. The islanders traded the spices with nearby countries for essential food such as rice. However, by the fifteenth century, Spanish and Portuguese sailors eager to find the source of eastern spices had discovered the Moluccas. By the seventeenth century the Dutch East India Company controlled the spice trade and the islanders. In order to stop the people selling to others, the Dutch cut down thousands of clove and nutmeg trees, ruining the livelihood of many. The islanders eventually rebelled and the company went bankrupt.

Indonesia today is still the world's largest producer of nutmeg, cloves, and pepper, although spices no longer have the value they had years ago.

NUTMEG

The nutmeg fruit grows on an evergreen tree. Inside the fruit is the red spice, mace, which surrounds the nut containing the nutmeg. Mace, which is a golden colour when dried, is used for savoury stews, and nutmeg flavours cakes and puddings. Other foods flavoured with nutmeg include sausages, pies, and soft drinks.

CLOVES

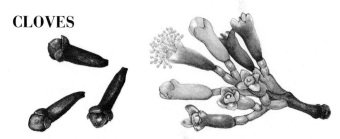

Cloves are the buds of a tropical evergreen tree. They may be used to flavour apple pies and cakes, but most clove oil is used in soaps, perfumes, and fillings for teeth! The Indonesians use cloves but not for eating – they make a clove cigarette called **kretek**.

PEPPER

This spice originally came from India, but the pepper vine is grown on a large scale in Indonesia and Malaysia. White and black pepper come from the berries which grow on spikes from the vine. Pepper is the most treasured of all the spices, and is used all over the world.

THE COCONUT

The Philippines (north of Indonesia) and Indonesia are the world's largest coconut-growing areas. The coconut fruit can float long distances across the sea and so the palm spread to sandy shores on many tropical islands. Today coconut palms are raised from the seed-nut and transplanted to large plantations.

The coconut palm is valuable in the Pacific islands, sometimes being a small island's only source of wealth. The coconut fruit has many uses:

Coir is the fibre from the outside husk. It is made into mats, ropes, and brushes.

The **shell** is made into bowls and ladles or used for fuel.

Coconut water, the liquid inside the shell, is a refreshing drink.

Copra is the dried white flesh inside the coconut, and the most valuable product.

Coconut oil is extracted by pressing the copra and is used to make margarine, cooking oil and soap.

Desiccated coconut, used in cakes and sweets, is made by drying and shredding the flesh.

HOW TO OPEN A COCONUT

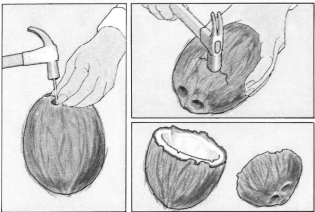

At the top of a coconut are three dark spots or 'eyes'. Pierce these with something sharp and drain out the coconut water. This makes a nice drink with fruit juice. Tap the back of the coconut with a hammer to crack the shell – it is best to do this outside. Prise out the white flesh with a blunt knife (take care not to cut yourself), then break the flesh into pieces.

For white grated coconut, peel off the brown skin before grating the flesh.

DID YOU KNOW?

The largest seed in the world is the **double coconut**, grown in the Seychelles, and weighing up to 18 kilograms.

Some farmers in Malaysia train monkeys to harvest the coconuts, teaching them to pick only the ripe nuts.

◀ GADO GADO ▶

This vegetable salad with peanut dressing is popular throughout Indonesia and can be eaten by itself or with a main meal and rice.

$\frac{1}{4}$ small white cabbage, finely shredded
100 g beansprouts, washed
2 potatoes, peeled and sliced
2 tomatoes, sliced
2 eggs
Sauce
1 tbs oil
1 clove garlic, crushed
1 fresh green chilli, finely chopped (optional)
2 tbs crunchy peanut butter
1 tsp malt vinegar
150 ml coconut milk (see next recipe)

1 Cook the eggs and sliced potato in boiling water for 10 minutes, then place in cold water.
2 Use the same boiling water to cook the cabbage and bean sprouts for 2 minutes. Drain them and rinse in cold water.
3 Slice the hard-boiled eggs and arrange the vegetables attractively on a large plate with the eggs on top.
4 **Prepare the sauce**: Heat the oil in a wok or large saucepan and stir-fry the onion, garlic, and chilli for 2–3 minutes.
5 Stir in the peanut butter, vinegar, and coconut milk and cook gently for a further 2–3 minutes.
6 Pour the hot sauce over the salad or serve separately in a jug.

Serves 4.

◀ COCONUT MILK ▶

This is made from fresh or desiccated coconut or may be bought as coconut cream, then diluted with water.

pieces of coconut flesh
or 200 g desiccated coconut
600 ml boiling water

1 Soak the coconut in boiling water and let it cool slightly.
2 In a liquidizer or food processor, blend the mixture together until it becomes a smooth paste. The milk may be used at this stage.
3 *Or* squeeze the mixture through a piece of muslin or a fine sieve to remove any bits.

◀ NASI GORENG ▶

This is one of the best-known dishes from the area. Muslims would replace bacon or ham with beef or prawns.

250 g dry long grain rice, cooked and cooled
1 medium onion, finely chopped
1 red chilli, seeded and finely chopped (optional)
1 clove garlic, crushed
200 g bacon *or* ham, chopped
100 g cooked chicken, chopped (optional)
2 tbs soy sauce
2 tbs vegetable oil

Garnish
1 egg
$\frac{1}{4}$ cucumber

1 For the garnish: Heat 1 tbs oil in a small frying pan. Beat the egg, pour into the pan, let it set and cook until golden. Turn over to cook the other side. Cut into strips and keep warm. Slice the cucumber.
2 Heat 1 tbs oil in a wok or large saucepan. Add the onions, garlic, and chilli. Stir-fry using a wooden spoon until the onion is soft.
3 Stir in the bacon or ham and chicken and cook for a further 2–3 minutes.
4 Add the soy sauce and the cooked rice. Toss and stir for another 3–5 minutes until the rice is heated through.
5 Serve on a warm dish, garnished with strips of omelette and slices of cucumber.

Serves 4.

◀ REMPAH ▶

Rempahs are a kind of Eastern hamburger with Indian spices. They may be eaten as a snack or served with rice.

250 g minced beef
$\frac{1}{2}$ grated coconut *or* 100 g desiccated coconut
1 clove garlic, crushed
$\frac{1}{2}$ tsp ground coriander
good pinch ground cumin
1 beaten egg
25 g cornflour
oil for frying

1 Soak the coconut in 4 tbs boiling water.
2 Mix the meat, squeezed coconut, and spices with beaten egg until the mixture sticks together.
3 Divide into 12 and shape into small burgers.
4 Dip each burger in cornflour, shake off the excess, then either fry or grill for 5 minutes each side. Serve hot.

Serves 2–4.

GRILLED CHICKEN
◀ **WITH COCONUT SAUCE** ▶

Chicken is a popular meat in Indonesia and this dish is served with a delicious lemon-flavoured spicy coconut sauce. Tamarind juice and lemon grass are traditional flavourings, but if they are difficult to find, use lemon juice and rind.

4 chicken portions with skin and fat removed
1 tbs tarmarind juice *or* lemon juice
salt
1 chicken stock cube
250 ml thick coconut milk (see page 93)
1 stalk lemon grass (optional) *or* lemon rind

Spicy mixture:
2 tbs vegetable oil
1 cm root ginger, peeled and grated
2 fresh green chillies, chopped and deseeded
2 onions, peeled and finely chopped
1 clove garlic, peeled and crushed
1 tsp ground turmeric
$\frac{1}{2}$ tsp each ground coriander and cumin

1 Rub the chicken pieces with salt and either tamarind juice or lemon juice.
2 Heat the oil in a frying pan and fry the spicy mixture for 1–2 minutes. Add the stock cube and gradually stir in the coconut milk. Bring to the boil, stirring with the lemon grass. Cook for 2–3 minutes, letting the lemon grass soak in the mixture. Remove the lemon grass and purée the mixture to a smooth paste in a food processor or liquidizer, *or* you may prefer the sauce with pieces in it.
3 Place the chicken portions, plump side uppermost, on a grill pan. Spoon some sauce over each one. Cook under a medium grill for 10–15 minutes. Turn the chicken over, spoon on some more sauce, then cook for a further 15 minutes.
4 Reheat the remaining sauce and serve with the cooked chicken portions. The dish may be served with rice and salad.

Serve 4.

JAVANESE
◀ **YELLOW RICE** ▶

500 g long grain rice
600 ml coconut milk (page 93)
or 150 ml milk + 450 ml water
1 tsp turmeric
1 chicken stock cube

1 Rinse the rice with cold water until the water is clear, to remove excess starch.
2 Drain the rice. Place all the ingredients in a large pan and boil. Stir the rice and cover with a tight-fitting lid. Lower the heat and cook gently for 20 minutes. If cow's milk is used, then stir occasionally to prevent sticking. Fluff the rice with a fork before serving.

Serves 4.

UNITED STATES OF AMERICA

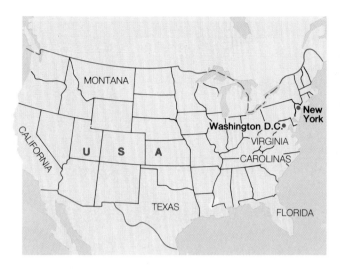

Chinatown, New York

Fifty states have joined together to form the huge country of the United States, a leading nation in industry and technology, with a population of 232 million. Each state has its own history, laws, and customs, as well as its own regional dishes.

HISTORY

The only people native to North America are the Red Indians and Hawaiians. The first settlement in the 'New World' was in 1607 in Virginia, and soon people came from all over the world.

Early English and Dutch settlers learned from the American Indians how to use local foods such as fish, maize, tomatoes, and wild turkey, and also pumpkin and squash which are vegetables like marrows. At first, the seeds the settlers brought with them did not thrive and the Indians saved them from starvation by showing them how to grow maize. Thanksgiving Day was a celebration of the first successful harvest and today it is the most important American holiday.

People spread westwards with the discovery of gold in 1849 and the Homestead Act of 1863 offered free land to settlers. Between 1880 and 1930 more than 27 million people had emigrated to the United States.

America today is a mixture of people from many cultures and Americans often identify themselves by the country of their forefathers, so there are Italian-Americans, Chinese-Americans, and Afro-Americans. Foods include dishes from around the world such as pizza, spaghetti, and chow mein, as well as dishes from North America such as New England chowder, creole jambalaya, and Boston brownies.

Americans like cooking outdoors on charcoal barbecues and also enjoy eating in the many fast-food restaurants which serve anything from hamburgers, fried chicken, and Mexican dishes, to ice-cream and doughnuts.

Barbecue, American style

AMERICAN FOODS AND FARMING

Wheat harvest, Montana

The United States is a rich agricultural land. It is the world's largest producer of maize, soya beans, and tomatoes, and the second largest producer of wheat, apples, oranges, and oats.
California in the West is famous for its fruit and vegetables, especially grapes, apples, and melons.
In the **Mid West** huge farms grow wheat, maize, sorghum, and soya beans, and cattle are reared.
The **East Coast** has a wonderful selection of fish, crustaceans such as lobsters, crayfish, and prawns, and shellfish, especially clams.
Florida in the South has huge citrus farms.
Rice is grown in the **Southern States**, especially Texas.

AMERICAN MEALS

Americans often enjoy a large breakfast of orange juice, pancakes with maple syrup, bacon and eggs, followed by a cup of coffee!
Lunch might be a snack meal of hamburgers, French fries, and salad, with a glass of milk.
The main meal of the day is in the evening. This might consist of fried chicken, peas, and mashed potatoes, followed by ice-cream with chocolate sauce and cookies.

DID YOU KNOW?

The United States holds some of the world's food production records:
The world's largest chicken ranch is in California, with 3 million hens producing $2\frac{1}{4}$ million eggs a day.
The White Sully, the heaviest type of chicken, is bred in California. A monstrous rooster called 'Weirdo' weighed 10 kilograms and was so ferocious that he killed two cats and crippled a dog!

Some of the world's heaviest fruits have been grown in America:
a lemon weighing nearly 4 kilograms and measuring 75 centimetres around the middle; a tomato of nearly 3 kilograms; a water melon weighing 90 kilograms.

Tapping sugar maple trees

Wild turkey

MAPLE SYRUP

The North American Indians tapped sugar maple trees in the spring when the sap was rising. The tree's bark was cut and buckets hung underneath to catch the dripping sap. The syrup was their only sweetener.

Maple syrup is made by boiling 40 litres of sap to give only one litre of syrup, so maple syrup is expensive. Americans use maple syrup to pour over pancakes and ice-cream.

RICE

In the United States, rice farms are the most mechanized in the world, using aircraft to set, fertilize, and spray the rice, and harvesters to reap the crop.

The story goes that a ship from Madagascar bound for England was blown off course and landed in Carolina for repairs. The people there were so kind that the captain left behind a bag of rice grains. Rice thrived in Carolina and an export trade soon developed. Rice production spread to other states and today American rice is exported to one hundred other countries.

TURKEY

The turkey came from Central America and spread in such numbers to North America that the American Indians could easily catch them to eat. In the sixteenth century, European explorers brought the turkey to Europe.

Turkey was part of the first **Thanksgiving dinner** held in 1621 when European settlers celebrated their first harvest in the new land.

SOURDOUGH

Over five thousand years ago the Egyptians found that flour left out in the open became wet and fermented, becoming bubbly. A lump of this 'wild yeast' dough or 'sourdough' was used to make bread rise.

The gold-rush of 1849 brought thousands of people to the west of America in search of gold. Sourdough pots were carried by the gold-miners and used to make light breads, pancakes, and an alcoholic drink called 'hooch'.

COCA COLA

Coca Cola was first made in 1886 by a man called John S. Pemberton, who sold it as a 'brain tonic'. The recipe is a secret but the drink consists mostly of water, sugar, and carbon dioxide to give the fizz. The special flavouring contains caramel and extract from cola nuts which is where the name came from.

BAKED BEANS

In America in 1895 someone had the clever idea of putting baked beans into cans. At first the cans contained a piece of pork, white beans, and tomato sauce. But now the recipe has changed and five billion cans are sold each year.

CORNFLAKES

An American, Dr Kellogg, invented a ready-to-eat breakfast cereal, cornflakes. He served them as a nutritious food for his patients and soon so many people wanted to try them that in 1902 a factory was opened for their manufacture. Today cornflakes are the most popular breakfast cereal in the world.

QUICK FREEZING

An American scientist, Clarence Birdseye, noticed when out on a hunting trip how the Eskimos left fish and deer to freeze very rapidly in the open air. When the meat was thawed it was tender and tasted like the fresh food.

After many experiments, Clarence invented a quick-freezing device which could freeze food at very low temperatures. Quick-frozen foods have smaller ice crystals which cause less damage to food when it is defrosted and so few nutrients are lost. Clarence's invention has changed shopping and eating habits all over the world.

ICE-CREAM

The Chinese are thought to have invented ice-cream some three thousand years ago. The first ice-cream factory was set up in Baltimore in 1851. Americans now each consume over 20 litres of ice-cream a year.

AT A COOL AND CHEERFUL PLACE
You'll find a wonderful girl in a real American pose ~ at the soda fountain ~ When thirsty remember her.

RE-FRESH YOURSELF! FIVE CENTS IS THE PRICE

Coca Cola advertisement, circa 1925

The original Kellogg's cornflakes packet

◄ HAMBURGERS ►

The original 'hamburger' came from Hamburg in Germany, but the Americans perfected the recipe, put the meat in a bun, and served it up with relishes and salads.

600 g lean minced beef
1 tsp each salt and pepper
2 tbs Worcestershire sauce
6 soft buns
6 dill pickles
3 sliced tomatoes
some crisp lettuce
mayonnaise and tomato ketchup

1 Put the meat and seasonings in a bowl and squeeze together using your fingers. Divide the mixture into six equal portions and pat *firmly* into six round hamburgers.
2 Turn the grill on to high and grill the burgers for 5 minutes each side.
3 Cut the buns in half and grill lightly.
4 Now build up the hamburger:
  Spread the bottom half of the bun with mayonnaise. Layer some lettuce, burger, tomato and sliced pickle on this. Spread the inside of the top of the bun with ketchup.
5 Serve with relishes and salad. Do not cut the bun – the skill is to eat it without spilling any!

Serves 4–6.

◄ CALIFORNIA SALAD ►

Fresh fruit and vegetables are plentiful on the West Coast where the weather is hot all year round.

½ Iceberg, Webbs, *or* other crisp lettuce
1 onion, thinly sliced
1 orange, peeled and sliced
1 grapefruit, peeled and sliced
25 g chopped walnuts *or* peanuts
3 tbs mayonnaise
1 small carton (about 150 g) of plain yoghurt
½ tsp each of salt and black pepper

1 Wash and shred the lettuce into bite-size pieces. Arrange in a bowl with the fruit and nuts. Add the onion.
2 Mix together the mayonnaise, yoghurt, and seasoning. When serving, pour some of this dressing over the salad.

Serves 4.

◄ CREOLE JAMBALAYA ► ◄ BOSTON BAKED BEANS ►

Creole cookery is a mixture from the many people who came to live in the South of the USA – French, Spanish, American Indians, and Africans.

Early settlers cooked huge pots of beans in their bread ovens for many hours. Traditionally, baked beans are eaten hot for Saturday supper, then cold for Sunday breakfast.

150 g long grain rice
1 large onion, peeled and chopped
2 tbs vegetable oil
1 medium green pepper, deseeded and chopped
200 g cooked ham *or* smoked sausage, cut into chunks
1 medium can (about 400 g) of tomatoes
250 ml water
½ tsp each of salt, pepper, and dried thyme
100 g cooked prawns
1 tbs chopped parsley, dried or fresh

1 In a large pan, heat the oil and fry the onion and rice until the onion softens. Stir in the ham or sausage, green pepper, tomatoes, thyme, seasoning, and water.
2 Boil, then cover and simmer for 25 minutes, stirring occasionally. Add the prawns and cook for another 5 minutes. The rice should be tender and the liquid absorbed.
3 Serve hot, sprinkled with parsley.

Serves 4.

500 g white beans (navy or haricot), soaked overnight *or* 2 cans white beans
1 tsp each of salt, pepper, and dry mustard
1 tbs molasses *or* black treacle
1 tbs brown sugar
8 rashers bacon, cut into chunks
1 onion, peeled and sliced

1 Put the beans in a large pan and cover with water. Boil, then simmer half-covered for 1 hour. (*Or* open the cans). Drain the beans and keep the liquid.
2 Set the oven at 160°C/325°F/Gas 3.
3 Put the beans in a large casserole and add the onion and the bacon. Mix all the other ingredients together with some bean liquid and make up to about 400 ml with water. Pour this over the beans and mix well. The liquid should just cover the beans.
4 Cover and cook in the oven for 1 hour, then uncover and cook for another hour. Add more liquid if necessary.

Serves 4–6.

◀ RED FLANNEL HASH ▶

This dish looks like its name and is a favourite 'Yankee' dish from the northern states, Serve hot with chutney, pickles, or ketchup.

3 large potatoes, peeled and chopped
25 g butter *or* 1 tbs oil
½ finely chopped onion
1 medium can (about 400 g) of beetroot *or* 2 cooked beetroots
1 small can (about 200 g) of corned beef
100 ml milk

1 Boil the potatoes in a large pan for 20 minutes until soft.
2 In a frying pan, fry the onion in the oil or butter for 5 minutes until soft.
3 Either drain the canned beetroot and chop, *or* peel the cooked beetroot and chop.
4 Drain, then mash the potatoes.
5 Mix together all the ingredients in the pan with the onion, and spread this 'hash' mixture evenly in the pan.
6 Cook gently until the bottom is brown and crusty. Serve hot.

Serves 4.

◀ CORN BREAD ▶

Hot breads are served with many meals in the South. They are often made from cornmeal and have names such as 'hush puppies' and 'spoon bread'.

100 g yellow cornmeal
100 g plain flour
25 g granulated sugar (optional)
4 level tsp baking powder
½ tsp salt
250 ml milk
1 egg
2 tbs vegetable oil

1 Set the oven at 220°C/425°F/Gas 7. Grease a 20 cm round cake tin *or* 12 bun tins.
2 Sieve together the flour, sugar, baking powder, and salt into a bowl.
3 Beat in the remaining ingredients to make a smooth batter. Pour into the tin and bake for 20–25 minutes until crusty and golden. Serve warm with butter.

◀ POPCORN ▶

Americans eat popcorn at any time of day, at the movies, at ball games, or at home. They usually serve it with salt and butter, but sugar may be used. Buy special popping corn.

100 g popping corn
1 tbs vegetable oil
½ tsp salt

▼

1 Heat the oil in a large saucepan and, when hot, add a little of the corn.
2 Quickly cover with a lid and shake the saucepan. Popping noises will start as the corn explodes and turns inside out. Continue shaking until the popping noises stop.
3 Remove from the heat and sprinkle with salt before eating.

BLUEBERRY-PATCH ◀ MUFFINS ▶

Blueberries grow wild in North America, but they may be bought in cans. Blackberries or blackcurrants can be used instead. Eat the muffins hot with jam.

100 g blueberries, blackberries, *or* blackcurrants – frozen, canned, or even jam can be used
250 g plain flour
50 g castor sugar
3 level tsp baking powder
½ tsp salt
1 egg, well beaten
250 ml milk
50 g butter *or* margarine, melted in a pan
1 tbs granulated sugar + 1 tsp lemon rind, grated

▼

1 Set the oven at 220°C/425°F/Gas 7. Prepare 12 paper cake cases *or* grease a bun tin. Wash and dry the fruit. Do not use sugar if jam is used.
2 Sieve the flour, sugar, baking powder, and salt into a bowl. Mix the egg, milk, and butter or margarine together, then stir quickly into the flour mixture using a wooden spoon. Gently fold in the fruit using a metal spoon.
3 Fill the cases or bun tins two-thirds full. Sprinkle the sugar and lemon rind on the top.
4 Bake for 20 minutes until golden brown, then remove and serve at once.

Makes 12.

THE WEST INDIES

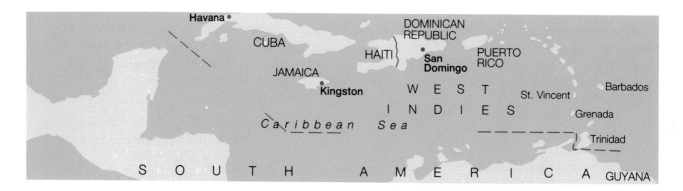

The West Indies are a chain of islands stretching for nearly 2000 miles between the mainlands of North and South America. They are part of the larger area called the Caribbean, which includes other islands such as Cuba and Hispaniola and gets its name from the Carib Indians who lived in the region.

Farming is the main source of wealth on these fertile tropical islands. Exotic fruits and vegetables are grown. Fruits include mangoes, coconuts, avocados, pawpaw, guavas, and pineapples. Breadfruit, cassava, plantains, yams, okra, and ackee are popular vegetables.

HISTORY

The Arawak and Carib Indians inhabited the West Indies long before Christopher Columbus made his journey in 1492 across the Atlantic Ocean from Spain. He thought he had discovered the Indies, so he named the islands the West Indies. Many battles were fought in later years for ownership of the islands. French, Spanish, Dutch, and British influences can be found all over the West Indies.

From 1518 until the nineteenth century many African slaves were brought over to work on the sugar plantations. With the abolition of slavery, people from India and China came to work on the islands.

Each culture brought new foods and their own special dishes. The Arawaks and Caribs lived by fishing and farming crops of cassava, yams, and sweet potatoes. Spanish explorers brought back tomatoes, maize, and peppers from South America. From Africa came okra, black-eyed peas, and groundnuts. People from India introduced rice, buffalo, and mangoes, and brought with them curry and chutney recipes.

WEST INDIAN FOODS

West Indian cooking is a 'melting pot' of foods from all the different peoples who have explored and settled in the islands. Exotic shellfish dishes and tropical fruits are eaten as well as simple soups and stews.

The islands have little grazing land, so pigs, which are easy to rear, are popular for meat. Thyme and bay leaves are used for flavour. Root vegetables such as yams and sweet potatoes are roasted or boiled to accompany meals. Fruit is plentiful and often eaten instead of puddings. Favourite drinks include fresh fruit juices, ginger beer, and, for special celebrations, rum.

West Indian recipes often have wonderful names. **Calaloo** is a well-known soup made from leaves like spinach. **Pepper pot** is a stew made from whatever ingredients are around and flavoured with a special ingredient called **cassareep**. This is made by squeezing the juice of raw grated cassava. **Jug jug** is a dish like a meat pudding and comes from Barbados.

Selling calaloo leaves at a market in Jamaica

SPICES OF THE WEST INDIES

Spices such as nutmeg, mace, ginger, cloves, cinnamon, and allspice all grow in the West Indies. Spices are such an important crop on Grenada that it is known as the Spice Island.

Most of the world's **allspice** comes from Jamaica. The green berries from the pimento tree turn black when dried. They have the flavour of cloves, cinnamon, and nutmeg – hence the name 'allspice'.

SALT FISH

Although the Caribbean seas had a plentiful supply of fish, the slaves had no free time to catch them. They were given supplies of preserved salt fish and used this with any available vegetables to make meals.

Today salt cod or ling fish is popular in West Indian cookery. The national dish of Jamaica is salt cod fish and the fruit ackee, cooked with onions, peppers, and tomatoes. **Metagee** is a salt fish and vegetable stew thought to come from Guyana, and the imaginative name '**Stamp and go**' is given to salt cod fish-cakes!

DID YOU KNOW?

The Arawak Indians gave us the name **barbecue**. They sliced meat into thin strips and laid it over an open fire covered with thin sticks called a **barbacoa**.

FRUITS AND VEGETABLES OF THE WEST INDIES

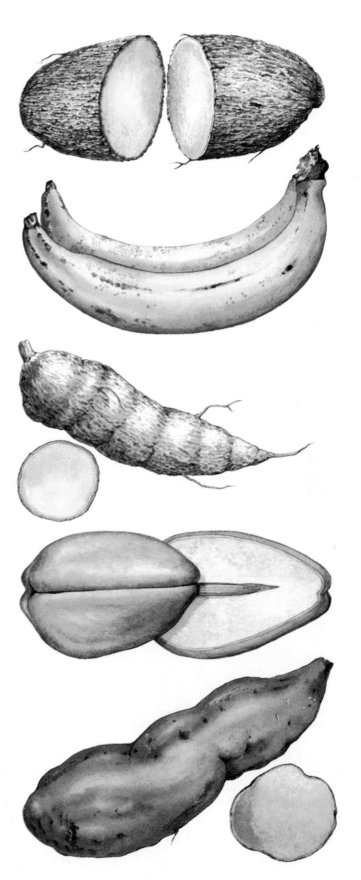

YAMS

Yams are root vegetables used a lot in West Indian cooking. The tough thick skin is removed and the yellow or white flesh is cut into chunks, then boiled for 20 minutes until soft. Yams are high in starch content but contain little else.

PLANTAIN

Plantains are a larger type of banana, less sweet and with tougher flesh, so they need cooking. Unripe green plantain can be boiled for 20 minutes as a vegetable, and ripe plantain fried for 10 minutes as a dessert.

CASSAVA

The root vegetable, cassava, is also called Manioc in some countries. The dark-brown hairy skin needs peeling before cutting the white flesh into chunks and boiling for 20–25 minutes. Some countries produce cassava flour and tapioca from the root.

CHRISTOPHENE

Christophene or chocho is a small greenish pear-shaped vegetable which when cooked tastes like courgette or marrow. Remove the skin, take out the central stone, and boil for about 10 minutes.

SWEET POTATO

The sweet potato is not really related to the potato. This root vegetable can be long or round. It has a pinkish skin and white or orange flesh. It can be peeled, chopped into chunks, and boiled for about 20 minutes, then mashed; or it may be roasted. The flesh tastes like sweetened potato.

BREADFRUIT

The breadfruit was brought from Tahiti to the West Indies in about 1790, by Captain Bligh of the Bounty. Plantation owners wanted the fruit as food for their slaves. The green warty rind needs peeling off, then the white flesh is chopped up before either boiling for 20 minutes or roasting or frying. Breadfruit gets its name because it tastes like bread.

ACKEE

Ackee is a fruit which is eaten as a vegetable and is specially popular in Jamaica. When ripe, the red fruits burst open, showing three black seeds on top of yellow fleshy 'fingers'. This flesh can be eaten fried or boiled for about 15 minutes. Ackee is also sold in cans.

MANGO

Mango with its thick green or yellow skin has pinky peach-tasting flesh and a large stone. Peel off the skin and remove the stone. The flesh can be eaten on its own or made into fruit salads or ice-cream.

SOUR SOP

The sour sop or sugar apple is a fruit which looks like a green spiny cone. To eat it, peel the skin, remove the pips, and suck the creamy flesh which tastes like a mixture of mango and pineapple.

PAWPAW OR PAPAYA

This is a yellowish fruit with sweet pink flesh and black seeds at the centre. Peel the skin and remove the seeds, then eat the fruit on its own or chopped up in fruit salad. **Papain** which is used to make meat tender, is obtained from the leaves of the papaya tree.

KING SUGAR

Loading sugar cane in Barbados

In India 2000 years ago, farmers grew sugar cane and knew how to extract sugar crystals from it. They passed the secret to the Chinese, who in turn told the people of Indonesia and their word 'shekar' gives us the English term 'sugar'.

Sugar cane was later introduced to Europe and in the fifteenth century Columbus took the plant with him to the West Indies. Thousands of slaves were transported from Africa to work on the plantations and sugar became the king of crops – the greatest industry in the world.

Once slavery throughout the British Empire was abolished in 1833, labour was difficult to find. During the war between France and Britain, Napoleon cut off the supply of sugar cane to Europe. It was then discovered that sugar could be extracted from sugar beet, grown in Europe. The West Indian sugar trade never returned to the boom times, but sugar is still the most important crop of the West Indies.

HOW IS SUGAR MADE?

Sugar cane is crushed, squeezing out the juice which is then concentrated by boiling. The refined sugar crystallizes out and is removed. Three or more boilings take place to remove more crystals, and the remaining syrup left after each boiling is called **molasses**.

NATURAL BROWN SUGARS

The West Indies produce several famous natural brown sugars, which must be made from unrefined cane in the country of origin.
Light Muscovado is creamy coloured and soft, with a little molasses in it.
Muscovado or Barbados sugar is soft, dark brown, and rich in molasses.
Demerara named after a district in Guyana has large golden sparkling crystals.
Molasses or Black Barbados is very dark, with a sticky texture and a toffee taste.
These sugars are used for their delicious flavour, especially in fruit cakes.

◀ METAGEE ▶

Salt fish such as cod or ling is an important flavouring in this fish and vegetable stew.

200 g salt fish
1 small coconut *or* 100 g desiccated coconut
450 g green plantains, peeled and chopped
100 g yams, peeled and chopped
100 g sweet potato, peeled and chopped
1 onion, sliced
1 tomato, peeled and chopped
sprig of fresh or dried thyme
4 okra (lady's fingers)

1 Soak the fish in cold water for 20 minutes.
2 Crack open the coconut, remove the flesh, and grate this into a bowl. (Desiccated coconut can be used instead.) Add 150 ml hot water. Squeeze the coconut in your hands to strain out the milk, then make up to 300 ml with water.
3 Place the vegetables in a very large pan and arrange pieces of fish on top. Add the thyme and coconut milk. Cover and cook for 20 minutes until the vegetables are soft. Serve hot.

Serves 4.

◀ PLANTAIN CHIPS ▶

In the West Indies plantain chips are eaten instead of crisps. Green plantains may be difficult to prepare since the skin can break off in pieces. Slice off both ends and cut the plantain in half. Make four slits lengthways and lift off the skin one strip at a time.

450 g green plantains
1 tablespoon salt
oil for deep frying

1 Peel and cut the plantains into very thin slices and soak them in salt water for 10 minutes.
2 Heat the oil in a chip pan. Remember not to leave the oil as it might catch fire. Drain the plantain and dry with a clean tea-towel. If the plantain sizzles in the hot oil, then it is ready for use. Fry a few slices for 3–4 minutes until they are crisp and golden.
3 Drain the chips on kitchen paper and sprinkle over a little salt.

Serves 4.

CURRIED ◀ GOAT WITH RICE ▶

The Indians who came to work in the West Indies brought with them their spicy recipes. Curried goat and rice is a popular Jamaican dish, but since goat is difficult to find, chicken may be used instead. West Indians often use a good curry powder instead of mixing the spices themselves. Use more or less chilli powder according to your taste.

700 g goat meat *or* 4 chicken portions
1 onion, peeled and diced
1 clove of garlic, peeled and crushed
1 heaped tbs curry powder
1 level tsp chilli powder
$\frac{1}{2}$ tsp each of salt and pepper
3 tomatoes, chopped
1 potato, peeled and diced
1 carrot, peeled and diced
2 tbs vegetable oil

1 Cut the goat meat into cubes or remove any feathers or fat from the chicken. Put either meat into a large bowl and stir in the diced onion, chilli, curry powder, garlic, pepper, and salt. Work the spices into the meat using your hands.
2 Heat the oil in a large heavy pan. Separate the meat or chicken from the onion. Fry small quantities of meat or chicken until the outside is sealed and beginning to brown. Remove, then fry the rest of the meat in the same way.
3 Put all the meat back into the pan. Add the onion and spice mixture, the chopped tomatoes, and enough water to cover the meat.
4 Boil the mixture, then lower the heat. Add the carrots and potatoes, then cover the pan and simmer until the meat is tender (goat may take up to 2 hours, chicken about 1 hour).
5 Taste the sauce before serving, adding more seasoning if necessary. Serve with boiled Basmati or long grain rice.

Serves 4.

In Jamaica a popular dish is 'rice and peas' made from red beans for 'peas', rice, and coconut milk. In Trinidad the people eat 'peas and rice', which is very different and made from dried peas, rice, onions, and tomatoes! This is the Jamaican recipe.

1 coconut *or* 100 g desiccated coconut
300 g long grain rice
1 medium can (about 430 g) red kidney beans
1 onion, peeled and finely chopped
sprig of thyme or dried thyme
$\frac{1}{2}$ tsp salt

▼

1 Crack open the coconut and remove and grate the flesh into a bowl, adding 150 ml hot water (or use desiccated coconut). Squeeze out the coconut milk with your hands and place in a pan.
2 Strain the beans and place in the pan with all the other ingredients. Add 600 ml water. Cover and cook gently until the water is absorbed. Serve hot.

Serves 4.

This spicy, moist cake is easy to make.

450 g sweet potatoes
25 g butter or margarine
75 g dark brown sugar (Muscovado or Barbados)
2 eggs, beaten
3 tbs milk
grated rind and juice of 1 lemon
1 tsp allspice *or* cinnamon
1 heaped tsp baking powder

▼

1 Set the oven at 180°C/350°F/Gas 4. Grease a medium loaf or cake tin.
2 Peel and slice the sweet potatoes into a saucepan. Just cover them with boiling water, then cover and cook for 20 minutes until soft. Drain, then mash them.
3 Beat in all the other ingredients. Pour the mixture into the tin and smooth down.
4 Cook for 40 minutes until a knife comes out cleanly. Cool, then turn out on to a wire rack.

MEXICO

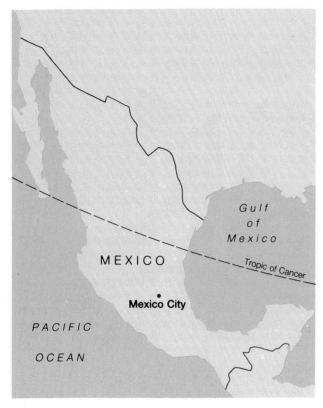

Mexico and a number of smaller states form a bridge of land between the continents of North and South America. Much of the land is dry and mountainous, especially in the north where wheat is grown and cattle raised. On the high plains, irrigation is needed to produce good crops of maize, and here sheep, goats, and chickens are farmed.

The Tropic of Cancer cuts across Mexico, so the south is tropical with good rainfall, growing crops of bananas, pineapples, and sugar cane. Mexico is the world's fourth largest producer of sugar cane.

HISTORY

Long ago wandering hunting tribes of American Indians settled in Mexico and developed farmlands and towns. They cooked simply, by boiling and steaming, and used wild ingredients such as turkey, pigs, tomatoes, beans, chillies, and maize.

When the Spanish invaded in 1519, they conquered and plundered a rich Aztec Indian civilization. The conquerors taught the Indians their language and customs and the Spanish introduced many foods including onions, garlic, sugar, wheat, and spices from the East.

Today Mexican cooking has a strong Spanish flavour spiced with Mexican chillies and served with the American Indian tortillas. The population speak Spanish and the majority are of mixed Indian and Spanish blood.

MEXICAN FOODS

CHILLIES

There are more than a hundred varieties of chilli pepper in Mexico. Some are mild, but others are extremely hot – young Mexicans measure their manliness by their ability to chew raw hot peppers. Remove the seeds to reduce the heat and always wash your hands after preparing chillies since they irritate the skin.

MAIZE

Maize or Indian corn is thought to have have originated from Mexico. The many kinds grown today were cultivated by the Mexican Indians long before the arrival of the Spanish. Maize is now the most important staple food in Latin America and grown on half the farming land in Mexico.

Maize is the main ingredient of the Indian pancake called the **tortilla**. The tortilla can be served in many ways:
When the tortilla is fried crisp and golden on both sides it is called a **tostada**. These are served covered with beans, cheese, and chilli sauce.
Tacos are tortillas curled into a shell shape and fried. Tacos can be bought ready-made, then warmed and filled with meat sauce such as picadillo and topped with salad and chilli sauce. Tortillas which are rolled up with onion and cheese inside, then covered with sauce, are known as **enchilladas**.

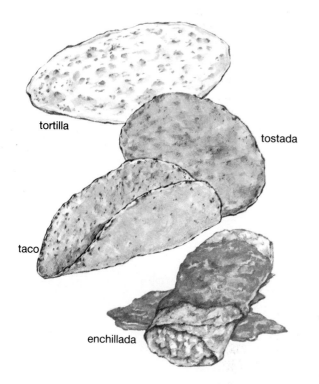

tortilla

tostada

taco

enchillada

Mexicans may eat as many as five meals a day although they usually have only three.

At sunrise a breakfast of buns with coffee may be taken followed later by a larger meal of eggs, beans, fruit, and tortillas.

A main meal of three courses is eaten around 3 p.m. and this may last several hours. It starts with soup or a tortilla dish, then there is a main course of meat or chicken, with beans, chilli sauce, salad, and tortillas, followed by fruit.

In the early evening there may be a meal of hot chocolate, biscuits, and fruit.

DID YOU KNOW?

I PUT THE CHOCOLATE IN AND NOTHING CAME OUT.

Cocoa beans were used as money by the Aztecs. Their Emperor, Moctezuma, had treasure rooms full of cocoa beans which he had made into jars of spiced **chocolatl**. For a century the Spanish invaders kept the secret of chocolate to themselves, but the French discovered the recipe and soon told the rest of the world.

Chilli con carne, made with chillies, minced meat, and beans, was invented in Texas. It was mistakenly thought to be Mexican.

◀ TORTILLAS ▶

Tortillas are served with all Mexican meals, and sometimes the tortilla is first used as a plate, then used to wipe the mouth, then eaten! In Mexico a special flour is used but a mixture of cornmeal flour and wholemeal flour produces similar results. Tortillas are fun to make, but be patient as it is a skilled job.

100 g fine cornmeal flour
100 g wholemeal flour
about 300 ml lukewarm water
a little oil

1 Place the flours in a large bowl and beat in enough water to form a dough. Knead the dough with your hands until it is smooth and elastic. Divide into 12 equal pieces.
2 Put a ball of dough between two pieces of lightly greased foil or greaseproof paper, about 20 cm square.
3 Roll the dough into a 15 cm circle.
4 Heat a lightly-greased heavy-based frying pan. Peel off one layer of paper and place the tortilla in the pan, paper side uppermost. Cook for $1\frac{1}{2}$ minutes. Remove the top paper, then turn over and cook for another $1\frac{1}{2}$ minutes until both sides are pale and dry.
5 Stack the tortillas and cover to keep warm.

◀ GUACOMOLE ▶

This delicious purée of avocados can be eaten with everything except dessert! Mexicans eat it with tortillas or tacos and it is a nice dip for raw vegetables.

1 tomato, peeled and finely chopped
juice of $\frac{1}{2}$ lemon, *or* 2 tbs lemon juice
2 ripe avocados
salt and pepper

1 Halve the avocados, remove the stones, and scoop the flesh into a large bowl.
2 Mash all the ingredients into the avocados with a fork. Season to taste.
3 Serve quickly to prevent the mixture from turning brown.

Serves 2–4 as a dip.

AVOCADOS

The avocado came from Central America and now grows in many tropical areas of the world.

The fruit is the size of a pear with an inedible green or blackish skin. To eat the fruit, split it open and remove the large stone. The pale green flesh may be eaten as it is or mashed and mixed with other ingredients. The avocado contains more protein and fat than any other fruit, as well as vitamins A and B-complex.

◄ PICADILLO ►

This savoury mince with almonds and raisins can be served with rice or eaten the Mexican way as a filling for tacos.

1 onion, peeled and finely chopped
500 g minced beef
1 clove of garlic, peeled and crushed
1 medium can (about 400 g) of tomatoes, with juice drained off
2 tbs tomato purée
50 g raisins
50 g almonds, chopped
salt and pepper

1 Cook the meat, onion and garlic in a heavy pan until the meat browns. The meat has enough fat not to need any more for frying.
2 Add all the other ingredients except the almonds and season well. Cover with a lid and simmer for 20 minutes, stirring occasionally.
3 Toast the almonds under the grill and scatter over the meat once it is cooked.

Serves 4.

◄ FRIJOLES REFRITOS ►

In Mexico, bean dishes are served at lunch, supper, and even breakfast time, usually with tortillas. This one has a strange name – it means 'refried beans', but it is only fried once!

1 can (430 g) kidney beans
25 g lard *or* 1 tbs vegetable oil
1 onion, peeled and chopped
2 tomatoes, peeled and chopped
1 small dried chilli, crumbled
salt and pepper

1 Heat the lard or oil in a pan. Fry the onion until it softens. Stir in the tomatoes and chilli.
2 Drain the beans, then add them to the pan. Stir and mash for about 10 minutes. Season well.
3 The finished dish should look like pink mashed potato and should be crisp underneath.

Serves 4.

SOUTH AMERICA

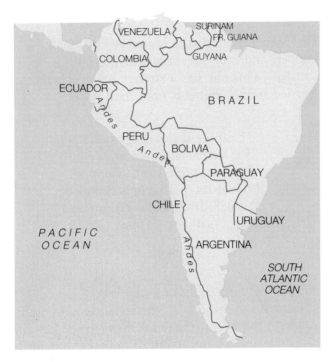

South America is a vast continent, two and a half times the size of Australia, with the 4000 miles of the Andes moutains stretching from north to south. Across the country there are great variations in climate and types of land, from deserts and mountains to tropical rain-forests and grasslands. Some areas have few roads or railways and communications are poor.

Cattle rearing in Argentina

HISTORY

When the continent was discovered by the Europeans in the fourteenth century, it was mostly inhabited by American Indians. Some, like the Incas of the Andes, were highly civilized. Today South America has the most mixed population in the world. There are descendants of the Indians, the Portuguese and Spanish adventurers, and the black slaves, brought from Africa to work the land. Spanish is the main language spoken, although in Brazil they speak Portuguese and in Guyana, English.

Each nationality has introduced its own foods and ways of cooking. The Incas brought maize from Mexico and skilfully farmed the crop in the high mountains. Maize is the most important staple food in South America, and is used for buns, soups, stews, and even drinks.

Foods originating from South America include potatoes, peppers, cassava, pumpkins, and some beans. Settlers planted sugar cane, coffee, bananas, wheat, and rice, and found they thrived. They introduced different types of farm animals, and great areas of grasslands in Argentina and Uraguay are used for cattle rearing. Food across the continent is varied and interesting, making use of ideas from all the different cultures and ingredients found in each region.

THE HISTORY OF THE POTATO

The South American Indians were eating potatoes 2,000 years ago. Little did the Spanish realize what treasure they had found when they took home the knobbly 'roots' grown by the Indians in the high mountains of the Andes. Only after several disastrous grain harvests in the seventeenth century did the people of Europe decide to plant potatoes. The descendants of those plants from the Andes form one of the most important crops in the world today.

How the potato has changed

TOMATOES

The tomato grew around the Andes mountains in South America and came first to Italy in the sixteenth century, but then soon spread to most parts of the world. It was known as the 'love apple' or 'Peruvian apple'.

Selling tomatoes, chillies, and limes in Ecuador

FREEZE-DRIED POTATOES

The Incas invented the first freeze-dried potatoes! They left potatoes out in the cold mountain air to freeze during the night, and in the hot sun by day to dry. The dried potato called **chuno** could be stored for several years, and provided food for winter.

WHAT ARE POTATOES MADE OF?

Potatoes consist of about 80 per cent water, 19 per cent carbohydrate, and small amounts of protein, vitamin C, and iron. If the skins are eaten they are a good source of dietary fibre.

DID YOU KNOW?

If Sir Walter Raleigh brought potatoes to England today, they might be banned, because green potatoes contain a poisonous substance called solanine. When potato plants were first introduced to the court of Queen Elizabeth I, the chefs served only the stems and leaves of the potato plant. These contain solanine and gave everyone stomach ache.

◀ PASTEL DE CHOCLO ▶

This traditional family dish from Chile uses savoury and sweet ingredients as well as locally grown maize (sweetcorn). The dish is usually made from chicken and beef, but for economy, only chicken has been included.

750–800 g of chicken pieces, with skin and
fat removed *or* 300 g cooked chicken
1 tbs vegetable oil
2 large onions, peeled and sliced
1 tsp each ground cumin and dried majoram
½ tsp each salt and pepper
1 heaped tbs flour
50 g raisins
2 hard boiled eggs
50 g black olives with stones removed (optional)
1 small can (about 200 g) of sweetcorn
2 eggs
150 ml milk
1 tsp sugar

▼

1 Cut up the raw chicken into smallish pieces and place in a large pan. Pour in some water then cover and simmer for 40 minutes (or cook in a pressure cooker for 15 minutes). Drain, cool, then remove the chicken meat from the bones. *Or* cut the cooked chicken into smallish pieces.

2 In another pan, heat the oil and fry the onion, spices, and herbs for 3–4 minutes. Stir in the flour, then add 300 ml water or, if ready, the water from cooking the chicken. Bring to the boil, then add the chicken meat and season with salt and pepper.

3 Set the oven at 200°C/400°F/Gas 6.

4 Put the chicken mixture into an ovenproof dish. Sprinkle the top with raisins, olives, and sliced hard-boiled egg.

5 Mix the sweetcorn, eggs, and milk together and pour this over the top of the pie. Sprinkle with the sugar and bake for 45 minutes until the topping has set.

Serves 4.

◀ EMPANADAS ▶

These little meat pasties, also called **empadas** or **empanaditas**, are popular all over South America, although they originated in Mexico. They are usually fried but the fat content is reduced by baking them.

200 g packet of frozen puff pastry (thawed)
or 200 g home-made puff pastry
Filling
(a) some picadillo (see p. 115)
(b) 100 g strong grated cheese, mixed with
1 chopped hard-boiled egg and 2 crushed
cardamoms
(c) 1 onion, finely chopped
200 g minced beef
1 tomato, peeled and chopped
1 small dried red chilli, crumbled
50 g sultanas
salt and pepper

1 For filling (c), place all the ingredients in a large pan and fry for 10 minutes, stirring occasionally. Remove and leave to cool on a plate.
2 Set the oven at 200°C/400°F/Gas 6.
3 Roll the pastry out on a floured surface, then using a saucer or cutter make eight 13 cm circles.
4 Place a tablespoon of the filling chosen on one half of each circle. Wet the pastry edges with water, fold over, and press the edges with a fork to seal them.
5 Place the pasties on a greased baking tray and cook them in the oven for 35 minutes. Remove and serve hot.

Serves 4.

◀ FLAN ▶

This caramel custard is one of the most popular desserts in South America.

75 g granulated sugar
400 ml milk
75 g castor sugar
3 eggs
vanilla essence

1 Set the oven at 180°C/350°F/Gas 4. Half-fill a roasting tin with water.
2 For the caramel, put the granulated sugar in a small saucepan and heat gently until the sugar liquefies and turns golden brown.
3 Pour the caramel into an ovenproof dish or 4 smaller dishes. Take care because the caramel is very hot.
4 Beat the eggs, milk, castor sugar, and a few drops of vanilla essence in a bowl, then strain through a sieve on to the caramel.
5 Put the dish into the roasting tin and cook in the oven for 25 minutes until the custard is firm – insert a knife and it should come out clean.
6 Chill the custard for 1–2 hours before serving. The small custards may be turned out on a dish, covered in the caramel sauce.

Serves 4.

JEWISH COOKING ▽△▽△▽△▽△▽△▽△▽△▽△▽△▽△

Judaism is the religion of the Jews, based on the teaching of Moses and other prophets of the Old Testament of the Bible. The Bible tells how Moses led his people from Egypt across the Sinai desert. On the way God gave them the Torah, the Book of Law, containing the ten commandments.

Throughout their history Jews have wandered from country to country and have often been mistreated. In the fourteenth and fifteenth centuries Jews were forced to leave Spain. They settled in other countries in Europe and around the Mediterranean. These Sephardic Jews make special dishes using recipes containing honey, rosewater, almonds, and sesame seeds.

In the seventeenth century more than half the Jews lived in Russia and Poland, so many traditional Jewish dishes reflect the cooking of these areas.

Today's 14 million Jews are scattered all over the world. America is the country with the largest Jewish population and three million Jews live in Israel.

JEWISH DIETARY LAWS

Kosher butcher's shop

Wherever Jewish people have settled they have used the local produce and adapted it to suit Jewish dietary laws.

One of these laws says that milk and meat must not be used together in cooking, or served at the same meal. Strict Jews do not eat food containing milk until three hours after finishing a meal containing meat.

Certain foods are forbidden. Meat may only be eaten from animals that have 'the cloven hoof and chew the cud', so pork is not allowed. This made good health sense, since when the Laws were made, pork meat could infect people with tapeworm.

Strict Jews eat only **kosher** meat that has been specially slaughtered.

Another law says that fish must have scales and fins, so shellfish and crustaceans are not used.

THE SABBATH

Preparing the Sabbath meal

The Jewish Sabbath begins at sunset on Friday and ends at sunset on Saturday. It is a day of rest and traditional households will allow 'no fire to be lit'. Long, slow-cooking dishes were invented which started cooking on the Friday and were eaten at lunch time on the Saturday. The whole family shares the Sabbath meal on Friday evening. The ceremony includes the lighting of candles and the saying of special prayers. A bread called **challah** is served. This is specially plaited and can be broken into pieces without the 'work' of a knife.

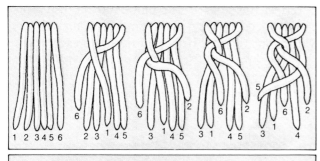

PASSOVER

Passover is a celebration of the exodus of the Jews from Egypt. In the rush to leave the country there was no time to ferment and cook bread. As a reminder, **matzos**, an unleavened crispbread which is quickly baked, is served during the eight days of Passover. **Matzo meal**, used in some cooked dishes, is made from ground matzos.

The Passover meal usually consists of traditional foods special to each family. In the centre of the table for the first meal is the **Seder plate**. This plate is arranged with special foods, each a symbol of Jewish tradition and history. Bitter herbs such as horse-radish, and green herbs such as parsley, are served on the Seder plate as a reminder of the 'bitterness of enslavement' and the suffering of Jewish people. The roasted egg and lamb bone represent the sacrifices which used to be taken to one great Temple in Jerusalem.

A Seder plate

Other holidays include **Pentecost**, seven weeks after Passover. The **Jewish New Year** is in September or October. Honey cake is served at this time. On the **Day of Atonement** the day ends with a meal of eggs, cheeses, and fish.

121

◀ CHOPPED LIVER ▶

For Jewish main meals some small dishes such as beetroot, olives, and chopped liver are served at the start of a meal.

100 g chicken livers
1 large onion, peeled and sliced
1 tbs vegetable oil
2 hard-boiled eggs
salt and pepper
chopped parsley

▼

1 Fry the onion in the oil until it turns brown. Chop the livers, stir them in, and cook for a further 5 minutes until tender. Season.
2 Either mince or use a food processor to turn the liver mixture and eggs into a smooth paste. Serve decorated with parsley.

Serves 2–4 as a starter.

◀ GEFILTE FISH ▶

Many of the Jews who migrated to Eastern Europe were very poor and lived during the week on a diet of potatoes, salted herrings, onions, and dark bread. The Sabbath was the day for fresh fish and by mixing the fish with other cheaper ingredients the dish could be stretched for several meals.

500 g white fish (cod, haddock, whiting, or coley)
2 onions, peeled and finely chopped
2 carrots, peeled and thinly sliced
2 eggs, beaten
4 heaped tbs medium matzo meal
(*or* breadcrumbs)
salt and pepper

▼

1 Cook the fish with a little onion and a little carrot in a saucepan with 500 ml water.
2 Remove the bones and skin from the fish. Mash or mince the fish, add the onions, salt, pepper, and eggs, and enough matzo meal or breadcrumbs to make a stiff mixture.
3 With wet hands roll the mixture into balls 3.5 cm in diameter.
4 Strain the fish stock to remove any bits and return the stock to the pan. Add the fish balls and sliced carrots. Cover and cook for 1 hour.
5 Lift out the fish balls and decorate each with a slice of carrot. Serve hot or cold with horseradish sauce.

Serves 4.

◀ CHEESECAKE ▶

Pentecost (Shevouth) comes seven weeks after Passover and was originally a celebration of the barley harvest. Later it was a reminder of when Moses gave the ten commandments to the people on Mount Sinai. It is the custom to eat cheese at the Pentecost festival in memory, it is said, of the Israelites who on returning to their camp after receiving the commandments found that their milk had soured and was turning to cheese. Cheesecake is a traditional dish served at the celebration.

125 g digestive biscuits
75 g butter or margarine
500 g cream or curd cheese
150 g castor sugar
3 eggs
juice of $\frac{1}{2}$ lemon *or* 2 tbs lemon juice
1 small carton (150 g) of natural yoghurt
2 level tbs plain flour

1 Set the oven at 180°C/350°F/Gas 4.
2 Put the biscuits in a bag and crush them into crumbs using a rolling pin. Beat the butter or margarine in a bowl until smooth, then work in the crumbs using a fork.
3 Use a 20 cm loose-bottom round cake tin or a deep flan dish. Press in the biscuit mixture and bake in the oven for 10 minutes.
4 Turn the oven to 190°C/375°F/Gas 5.
5 Prepare the filling. Put the eggs and sugar in a large bowl and, using an electric or rotary whisk, beat for 5–10 minutes until thick and creamy.
6 In another bowl mix together the cream cheese, flour, lemon juice, and yoghurt. Spoon in some of the egg mixture, then add the rest. Pour on to the biscuit crust and bake for 45 minutes or longer until firm and golden brown.

INDEX OF RECIPES

INDEX

EDUCATION